One Brave Heart

The Geoff Fisher Story

Eve Creed

 A catalogue record for this book is available from the National Library of Australia

Copyright © 2022 Eve Creed
All rights reserved.
ISBN-13: 978-1-922727-45-9

Linellen Press
265 Boomerang Road
Oldbury, Western Australia
www.linellenpress.com.au

Dedication

This biography/memoir has only been possible due to the good-humoured, generous and candid collaboration between Geoff, wife Toni, sister Robyn, and sister-in-law/author Eve.

Geoff's story is primarily dedicated to his children, Emma, Brendan, Jasmine, Ashley, and his grandchildren Charlie, Max, Forrest, and any who may be born in the future. It is also dedicated to Geoff's sisters, Janis and Robyn, and extended family members who would like to know more about his personal history.

He believes all his good friends deserve recognition, but special dedication is reserved for friend Robert Larbalestier – for a friendship that Geoff will always hold very dear.

Acknowledgement

Heartfelt thanks to Geoff's Mardon-family cousin, Maxine Tapper (nee Williams) for sharing her precious collection of family photographs and helpful information related to them.

Geoff also acknowledges those who gave him nature and nurture – his parents, Henry Fisher and Jessie Fisher (nee Mardon), with all their siblings and parents before them.

Contents

Dedication iii
Acknowledgement v
Contents vii
Introduction 1
Chapter One - First Meeting 7
Chapter Two - Beginnings 9
Chapter Three - My father's background 10
Chapter Four - Boulder home 15
Chapter Five - My mother's background 20
Chapter Six - First Collie home 22
Chapter Seven - Second Collie home 24
Chapter Eight - My coal mining town 27
Chapter Nine - Self-Sufficiency 31
Chapter Ten - Fisher food 37
Chapter Eleven - Swimming: Part one 44
    Swimming: Part two 47
Chapter Twelve - Bikes 50
Chapter Thirteen - My primary school years 54

Chapter Fourteen - My high school years ... 72

Chapter Fifteen - High school ups and downs ... 80

Chapter Sixteen - More about Henry ... 89

Chapter Seventeen - More about Jessie ... 99

Chapter Eighteen - A bit about siblings ... 108

Chapter Nineteen - Moving on ... 114

Chapter Twenty - Freelancing ... 126

Chapter Twenty One - More of Adelaide and Alice - and Therese ... 141

Chapter Twenty Two - Back to Perth ... 145

Chapter Twenty Three - Partnerships, Pools and Waters Beyond ... 151

Chapter Twenty Four - Men in Lycra ... 156

Chapter Twenty Five - Destiny ... 159

Chapter Twenty Six - The wedding – and family ... 172

Chapter Twenty Seven - Revisiting Collie ... 184

Chapter Twenty Eight - Studio changes ... 188

Chapter Twenty Nine - A scare at home ... 195

Chapter Thirty - Medical relationships ... 198

Chapter Thirty One - Optimism ... 201

Chapter Thirty Two - The joy of travel ... 208

Chapter Thirty Three - Life at home ... 212

Chapter Thirty Four - Fitness, friends, and more ... 214

Chapter Thirty Five - An unforgettable event ... 217

Chapter Thirty Six - Cardiac Unit 223

Chapter Thirty Seven - Legs 227

Chapter Thirty Eight - Neurological Ward 230

Chapter Thirty Nine - Shenton Park Rehabilitation Hospital 234

Chapter Forty - Let there be light 240

Chapter Forty One - Studio concerns 245

Chapter Forty Two - Being a survivor 247

Chapter Forty Three - Ablations 263

Chapter Forty Four - Fiona Stanley Hospital 270

Chapter Forty Five - On the list 274

Chapter Forty Six - And there was more 277

Chapter Forty Seven - A most momentous day! 282

Chapter Forty Eight - Meanwhile in ICU 285

Chapter Forty Nine - The good and the bad of post-op 287

Chapter Fifty - Joy 292

Chapter Fifty One - Reflections 295

Chapter Fifty Two - Donate Life and donors 298

Chapter Fifty Three - Music's in the heart 300

Chapter Fifty Four - Life post-transplant 302

Chapter Fifty Five - A message to my children and grandchildren 305

Chapter Fifty Six - Covid 19 and more reflection 307

A few extra family pics *310*

Some of Geoff's arty photos	*311*
Venice	*313*
NOT THE END!	*315*

Introduction

This story is about my brother-in-law, Geoff Fisher. He represents many Australian men in many ways, but he is also unique. I have witnessed his free spirit driving him to reach his goals, pushing through life's obstacles and rising above them to create positive life experiences. The purpose of this biography is to attempt to communicate the essence of this man and some of his life journey.

My introduction is quite lengthy because Geoff is one of earth's complex characters, but I have come to understand him well over time and have a desire to share this with others.

As a novice biographer, I am also interested in how an individual's history impacts his or her life, lived within a cultural framework in ways that often cannot be fully understood by other generations or other cultures. Yet, it is extremely important to consider how our personalities, talents and interests are affected by our shared ancestral DNA. Research into Geoff's family background has helped build more understanding of Geoff's nature/nurture influences during his growing years. Unfortunately, research into his parents' and grandparents' backgrounds have hit some genealogical 'brick walls', leaving many questions unanswered.

Biographies are important because younger generations frequently do not think to ask their parents, grandparents or other relatives many deep, searching questions about their lives. In addition, 'children' of any age tend to view their parent only as a parent, unaware of his or her range of complex experiences from birth through to adult years, particularly before he or she became a parent. It is often not until a parent or relative dies that we realise how little we have known about that person's character and history, as well as about their forebears. Of course, this can apply in any relationship. In some cases, few records have ever been created or have been lost, and then it is often too late to learn.

Geoff is an Aussie man, an individual who does not seek to satisfy the expectations of others. He is 'his own person' and lives by his own standards, desires and needs. At odd times, he may express this characteristic somewhat selfishly. Yet, he is also open to receiving criticism. When such criticism seems justified, after considering the reasons given and fairness involved, he adjusts his behaviour to meet the needs of others accordingly – otherwise, he does not. Sometimes he quietly assesses his own behaviour and addresses his fault. He generally respects someone who speaks their mind, even if not in his immediate favour, given that they are not abusive, uncaring or simply power-seeking.

Regardless, he loves and cares for those who have been and are presently close to him. He also creates opportunities to get to know others in his environment with a strong sense of being in a community of other individuals – rather than in a tribal mass. He is not interested in decorating himself with designer label clothes or tattoos, swearing, or other 'tribal' things, but he does enjoy being in sporting teams and sharing in creative groups. He regards and treats women with equal respect and affection as men. He is not afraid of rejection, believing it is always worth trying to develop relationships even if others are initially reserved or resistant, and then it is up to them to respond. There is no limit to his friendships, as he is so gregarious. He prefers to see the best in others, unless and until they prove otherwise – and usually more than once.

Because of his own positive attitude, at times he can become frustrated, impatient and critical of others who express negativity or have a 'can't do' attitude. However, if it is within his power, he is eager and willing to show or explain how something can be done, or at least investigated. One of his mottos could be, 'If you don't try, you'll never know!' This behaviour can appear patronising, or dismissive of the other's feelings in the moment. Geoff competes mainly with himself, except in team sports and for fun.

Those who know Geoff, also know that he is idiosyncratic and contradictory. He is very curious and creative, with a good dose of rebellion and stubborn independence. He acts with a high degree of spontaneity and impulsivity. He has a sharp, quick, and often distracted mind – sometimes known as a 'monkey mind' – which can cause some tasks to be delayed or forgotten, yet can lead to amazing, fresh ideas and experiences. (The process can also drive others temporarily crazy!) Admittedly at times, some very specific, positive experiences are completely forgotten or diminished in his memory, but equally, some very bad experiences are completely forgotten or diminished in his memory … his mind has simply moved on with other 'forward' things in life! Nevertheless, he never forgets people who have shared his life, crossed his path or have been important to him in some way. People matter to him in all areas of his life, and he is happiest when interacting and sharing with others. His pets have mattered greatly too.

Geoff actively learns by 'doing', but he frequently appears to have learned intellectually by 'osmosis'. Quietly listening and observing all kinds of facts and details, he learns about surprisingly diverse things that are interesting or meaningful to him.

A clever, irrepressible sense of humour regularly intersperses his interactions, unless he is feeling particularly stressed or, on occasion, depressed. At times, he combines his humour with intriguing knowledge expressed in innovative language, in surprising statements such as, "I see life through my vitreous humour!" Of course, there's always a meaningful link in his mind, an 'out of left field' vision, not always obvious to others in the moment.

Yet there's more to tell. Geoff's story evolves to reveal his greatest challenge, proving more of his resilient character. He is a man with a huge spiritual heart. He is worth knowing and his life is worth knowing about.

Geoff's biography has been created through a series of face-to-face interviews. During all interviews he has been willing, generous and open about difficult and painful events, while also sharing a wealth of amusing, and rewarding experiences. His wife and sister have also contributed greatly, as essential characters in his story, so much is revealed of them too – fortunately they are natural oral story-tellers in their own right. Geoff's story naturally involves much of his Fisher family, but it is also interwoven with my family. As the interviewer, collator and writer motivated to create this project, I have some inevitable bias and input. We recognise that experience and memories all come from a different perspective. Nevertheless, in our collaborative effort, we have all done our best to relate events honestly, checking facts and memories wherever possible within our limited time frame and recall.

We have included many photographs, some in their

authentic 'untidy' condition, as vital windows into aspects of Geoff's life – and the past – even before his birth. Thank goodness for precious photographs!

Already, Geoff has noted that there are more valued experiences and characters he has not been able to include. Geoff's memories seem to constantly bubble up from a rich, bottomless well of life, but we have had to limit interviews and anecdotes in order to reach a point of writing completion.

Chapter One

First Meeting

I am writing about a man who I did not enjoy meeting, initially, in spite of his impressive appearance. I met him when he was feeling angry and upset.

This man is Geoffrey James Fisher. He presented himself at his close friend-and-colleague Ric (Richard) Syme's family home, on Christmas Day, 25th December 1982. My sister Toni and I, and our mother Anne, were already there. I had at one time been married to Ric's brother, and for various reasons our two families were able to come together for the Christmas affair – a rare event!

While we were all communing and imbibing happily, Geoff appeared at the front door – standing tall in stature, slim, well dressed, clean shaven, very handsome. Yet, he also stood at the threshold with a heavy, sombre expression. I thought his face 'looked like thunder' and was not thrilled to meet him. At the same time, Toni and Mum (Anne) were immediately captivated.

An already jovial, celebratory mood, enhanced by the seeming limitless flow of champagne, allowed a different vision for them, but it did not greatly alter my own view. We three – Toni, Anne and I – were enjoying our cigarettes in fashionable tar-guard cigarette holders, considered the responsible, healthy option at the time, and we felt quite sophisticated. So ... Geoff entered Ric's large, open lounge room, with everyone already revelling in the bubbly joy of Christmas, cigarette smoke floating and swirling upward and around us all. Animated, excited chatter filled the expansive room.

Moments before Geoff arrived, Ric had briefly informed us that he had invited his friend to join us. He told us that Geoff was unable to spend the day with his little children in their family home because his recent ex-wife wanted it that way. Geoff responded positively to Ric's invitation, needing friendship that day. Well, he certainly found that, and more! None of us could have imagined the consequences of that meeting as he stepped over the threshold. Nor could any of us, seeing this embodiment of fitness, strength and vitality, have imagined the challenge he would face much later in life.

Before resuming the story about points at which our lives came together and were shared, it is essential to learn about Geoff's origins and earlier life to get to know him well.

Chapter Two

Beginnings

"Right, well, I was born in Kalgoorlie Hospital on the 3rd of August, 1947. But before that great event, my mother fell off her bike when she was heavily pregnant with me, and I say that accounts for a lot of things!"

Our interview had begun before I had time to turn on my recorder, or to get my notepad ready. This is how most of our interviews began, and I laughed every time.

Geoff was born in Kalgoorlie Hospital because his father, John Henry Fisher, worked in the Kalgoorlie/Boulder shire as a gold miner at the time, and lived in Boulder. He always used the name 'Henry', rather than John. In 1939, twenty-nine-year-old Henry married twenty-one-year-old Jessie Edith Mardon. Jessie's family lived in Cue in the Goldfields at this time.

Jessie's mother Daisy Phillips (far right) as a young girl at home with her family in Day Dawn – now a ghost town – near Cue in W.A., early 1900s

Chapter Three

My father's background

"My father, Henry, came to Australia from England, basically as child-labour, in his teens. He later worked on farms around Esperance and Scaddan and places like that in Western Australia. Then he went mining in Kalgoorlie, then Collie."

Henry was born 'John Henry Fisher' on 27th August 1910 in County Durham, in the north-east of England. We know that he left Durham in November 1927, having recently turned seventeen, as he set sail alone from London for the Western Australian port of Fremantle on the P&O Line steamship *S.S. Bendigo*. Henry identified himself as a garden boy on the British passenger embarkation list. The ship typically sailed from London, around the Cape of Good Hope, over great expanses of precarious waters and onward to Australia. The journey took the usual month to complete.

The setting from which Henry emigrated is important to understand. In Britain's post-World War I in the 1920s and 1930s, there was a steady decline in its previous economic strength, as it fell into depression, unemployment, deflation and poverty. County Durham had around 200 coal mines, many of which had to close with severe cuts to miners' wages or complete loss of work. Strikes and protests were common. Henry's father was a coal miner, so all of their futures were likely to be uncertain. In the First World War, Australia lost many men, so during the 1920s and 1930s, its workforce was still severely depleted. At this time, Australia had some of its own serious post-war economic problems, but it was also expanding with opportunities in the countryside, needing to develop and farm vast areas of virgin land.

These conditions brought about a scheme, arranged between the British and Australian governments to emigrate children and youths to different parts of Australia in order to work the land. Many different organisations in Australian States ran separate programs to administer the overall scheme. Young newcomers' ship transport was sponsored in various ways, with some having to repay travel costs over time to their program sponsors.

Within these programs, various forms and quality of supervised care and training in agricultural farm schools were provided, promising to educate and lead them into employment. Younger children were managed by different organisations to those managing youths in the sixteen to twenty-year-old age group.

With very few work prospects in England and greater opportunities on the horizon, Henry took his chance. No doubt it was hard for his parents and younger brother Joseph to say goodbye. Later, on 19th February 1929 at only sixteen years of age, Joseph followed Henry out to Australia on the Ormond. On the British passenger embarkation list, Joe identified himself as a dairy farmer. He also travelled alone, except for the many other young men on board seeking a similar new life.

Because of his young age, like his older brother Henry, it is likely that 'Joe' came here under a similar farm school scheme. He met up and worked with Henry at various points in time, but exactly where, when and how are unclear.

The present Fisher family do not know the specific program in which Henry participated, so do not know where his life started in WA. Efforts to find information through early training records in WA have come to nought. Henry simply told Geoff – resentfully – and more than once, 'We were just slave labour!' However, he told his youngest daughter, Robyn, a few times that he had been a stowaway on the ship at the age of fifteen. That seems to have been an entertaining 'red herring', of sorts. Official ship arrival records prove that Henry was seventeen. About his early arrival and consequent experiences, Henry kept his cards very close to his chest.

Henry arrived in Fremantle on 31st December, 1927. It was New Years' Eve. He was about to start a completely new life in a new country in a new year. We may wonder if he held serious regrets as he landed at Fremantle Port to a very foreign landscape, without family or old friends. Yet, we may also wonder if, as a male youth, he held great expectations with a positive desire to better his prospects and a strong sense of adventure.

Henry Fisher - after arrival in Australia, 17 years old (?)

Brothers Joe and Henry (L to R) with dog on railway cart (c. 1929-1932) Likely in Scaddan/ Esperance area in WA.

Young Henry Fisher working the land, with dog c.1929 – 32

This was taken the sunday after a dance from wich I did not get home till half past five and up befor nine

Henry

Written on back of previous photo

Chapter Four

Boulder home

In 1939, when Henry married Jessie Mardon, they made their family home at 111 Federal Road in Boulder, in a typical, basic, small weatherboard mining house with 4 rooms and a corrugated tin roof – much the same as the last home Jessie had lived in with her family in Cue.

Front view of 111 Federal Road, Boulder 1939
With Jess and Bill, the dog.

Back view of Federal Road, Boulder
House just built.

Henry and Jessie – honeymooning (?) c.1939-1940

Geoff notes: "Our favourite photo of our parents before we were born – woollen bathing costumes in the 1940s made a fashion statement!"

Jessie, Henry and Alan, again in the tyre tube at Esperance beach, 1942
– wearing more modern bathing attire!
(Henry likely on leave from army base in Cowra, NSW)

Alan (3 yrs.) with Jessie on her trusty bike. Boulder 1942

Boulder borders Kalgoorlie in the gold mining territory of Western Australia – an area of 'gold rush' history with its own harsh mining stories and ghosts with tales to tell. The house was placed on some bare, dusty, red earth with an unnamed road near a mine, described by Geoff as "just past the tailings dump". In 1947, Geoff was born in Kalgoorlie Hospital, while at home, seven-year-old Alan was waiting to meet his new baby brother. When Geoff was 18 months old, both he and Alan met their next sibling, baby sister Janis.

One of Geoff's earliest memories of his home as a toddler was of watching Alan and his friends going out the back gate that led directly onto an overburden.

"I remember watching my brother Alan, and his friends, skidding down the overburden on sheets of cardboard or tin. I tried to do it too. Overburden is the dumped top soil removed from the surface of a gold mining site. But I was petrified of a cow there, that seemed to walk over me as I cowered on the ground against a corrugated iron gate. Obviously, it knew to walk around me, but it was pretty terrifying because the cow was huge and I was small. It appeared monstrous to me as a toddler.

"But the house was also surrounded by trees with kookaburras, crows, magpies, and more, as well as rabbits, kangaroos, snakes and lizards, and all kinds of wildlife. It was actually quite idyllic for kids."

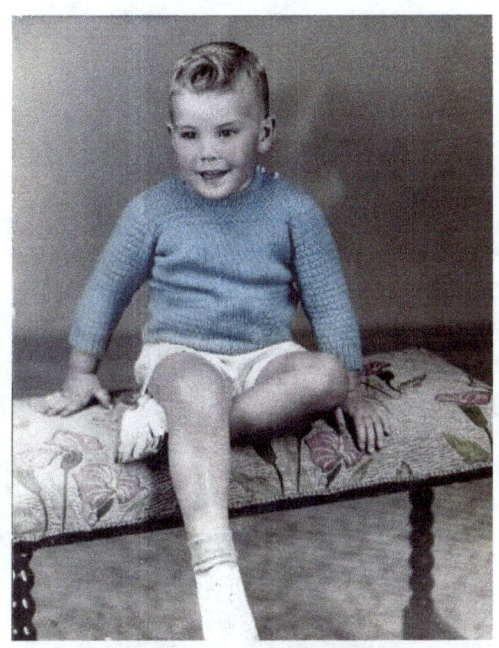

Geoffrey James, 3 years old, Boulder (1950)

It was in Kalgoorlie that Geoff's love of swimming manifested at the age of three. "I have a fond memory of being taken by my parents to Kalgoorlie's town swimming pool – with its modern tiles. Hanging onto the side of the pool, I felt happy and secure in the water."

Surprisingly, Kalgoorlie's swimming pool was the first Olympic-size 50 metre pool built in 1938 in WA, during a time of great prosperity. It was also the second Olympic pool built in Australia. It was intended to provide first class opportunity for competitive sport and recreation for people living in the Goldfields.

Geoff continues, "Also from around the age of three, in Kalgoorlie, I have a vague memory of Arthur Mardon, my maternal grandfather, silhouetted against the morning light filtering through the back door of the house ..."

Chapter Five

My mother's background

"My mother's maiden name was Jessie Edith Mardon."

Jessie's professional portrait photograph,
taken at Perth's prominent Lafayette Dease Studio

To understand a little of Jessie's character and subsequently her influence on Geoff's character, we can consider her own ancestry. Jessie's Mardon ancestors were originally from the south of England. They were Unitarians, a non-denominational religious group that emphasised freedom and tolerance in religious belief. They believed salvation should be extended to all mankind. In the context of their time, this represented a very free and open belief system which had emerged from the 'Non-Conformist' religion. It seems non-conformism has been embedded in the Mardon descendants' DNA!

Jessie appears to have expressed much of her father's – Arthur Mardon's – qualities. Arthur was born in South Australia, but at some point, his family moved to Cue in the WA goldfields. This is where, at age twenty-two, he met and married Daisy Phillips who was just nineteen. Arthur had played and competed in the Boys' Brass Bands successfully for several years before he met Daisy, and he continued to be a dedicated brass band player throughout his life. An untitled photo also shows him as a member of a football or rugby club as a youth, where he appears to have a strong body and happy to be in a competitive team.

Arthur and Daisy had three daughters, Jessie, Dorothy (Dot) and Beryl. Jessie was their first child, born in Perth in 1918, the last year of the First World War.

Mardons (L to R) Dorothy, Jessie, mother Daisy, Beryl
Kalgoorlie 1938-40

Chapter Six

First Collie home

When Geoff was just four years old, in 1951, his maternal grandfather, Arthur, died of a heart attack at the age of sixty-two. He was living in Perth at the time, but it seems this event may have contributed to the Fisher family's decision to move from Boulder to Collie. Collie, a small coal mining and timber felling town in the South-West region of Western Australia, has always had the only coalfields in Western Australia, providing power for the State

John Henry Fisher, who preferred to be known as 'Henry', chose to move his family to this more sedate, greener part of Western Australia, and to change his occupation from gold miner to coal miner.

Geoff noted, "He decided there were better work prospects in Collie." Although coal mining was central to County Durham where he was born and raised, he may also have been prompted to move because he and Jessie had three young children to raise, and Collie could offer a more nurturing environment at that time.

Their first small home was a miner's cottage on land just east of the Collie township, within the immediate area of the Cardiff coal mine where Henry secured his first job. It was so close to the mine that from his home, little Geoffrey could walk to the pit and watch the men and ponies going in and coming out of the mine.

"I enjoyed watching the ponies going down the coal pit incline with chaff bags attached to their heads, returning with skips full of coal. I also watched the trains hauling coal away from the mine and into Collie."

However, the Fishers' home was much too small for a growing family, so Henry soon moved them to a larger one.

Chapter Seven

Second Collie home

The Fishers' second home was at 24 Ogden Street in the town. It was a typical miner's and timber-feller's square, four-roomed, jarrah weatherboard cottage with a corrugated iron roof on a quarter-acre block, much like their house in Boulder. Its basic layout consisted of four main rooms. On the right side were the lounge and one bedroom, on the left side were the kitchen and one bedroom. The bedrooms were at the front of the house. Attached to the back of the kitchen, on the left side of the back verandah, was a small bathroom-laundry. Soon, a small 'sleepout' was attached on the right side of the back verandah, in this case more solid than most, built with Besser bricks to waist height, with louvred windows above - very common in the 50s and 60s as a vital form of ventilation control.

The front door was inset with a popular leadlight glass design, and Geoff fondly remembers, "As a child, I enjoyed observing its odd shapes and imperfect glass."

The floors were timber, the doors were timber, the walls were timber. As Collie was set amongst dense jarrah forests, the sturdy, hardwood jarrah timber – now so admired, so expensive, and endangered – was readily available. Consequently, surrounding native hardwood trees were exploited for most buildings.

"The ceilings were comfortably high at about 11 feet. I remember that the lounge room inner walls had black, vertical boards that went from the floor to about a man's waist height, like the miners' houses in Kalgoorlie/Boulder.

"The 'dunny' was way up the back yard. There was also a work shed at the end of the yard which doubled as a horse stable."

The Dunny

The popular slang 'dunny' for toilet comes from the original British 'dunniken', derived from 'dung', and 'ken' meaning 'little house'. The outside 'dunny' holds many childhood memories for Geoff.

"There was a large can placed under the toilet seat for everyone's 'business', along with pieces of newspaper or scrap paper used – because toilet paper was not on our shopping list in those days. The can was collected weekly by the 'night-cart' which was driven down everyone's back lane, and from there the can was retrieved from a special outlet at the back of the dunny. The smell of strong carbolic disinfectant was overwhelming. The cans became rusty and leaky in time too. We were told that once a night-cart man hoisting a can up to his shoulder suffered the indignity of the contents leaking all over him. We thought that was hilarious!"

Yet, going to use the dunny wasn't so funny. "It was as far away from the house as possible. We had to go up the garden path, through a gate, past the chook yard, under the mulberry tree and beyond, with a hurricane lamp at night, in any weather. There was a shed-come-horse-stable for Alan's horse up there too. As we hurried there, shadows ran with us, creating scary moments! And in warmer months, fumes wafted down from the dunny, magnifying the carbolic disinfectant. In those early days, a flushing toilet was in the realm of science fiction."

Chapter Eight

My coal mining town

"As a child, living near the coal mine, I used to see steam trains going by the back fence. I used to break off bits of grass tree, and put them on the line, or a penny, just for the excitement of what could happen … and, of course, they got flattened!

"What I remember of the coal mine was the little railway going down an incline, disappearing into the darkness. In the cold, foggy, frosty mornings, I'd go to the entrance of the mine and watch the ponies appearing out of the darkness, with miners wearing carbide lamps on their helmets, a thing of the distant past these days. The lamps held a greenish-grey powder and a little water tank. Drops of water on the powder made the gas, which created a flame when ignited. The horses had bags of chaff attached to their heads so they could eat while they were working. Having an incline, the miners and ponies had to walk down into the mine, load the skips with coal by hand and walk back out. As teenagers, we ventured down another coal mine at the edge of town but we didn't go very far because it scared the hell out of us.

"Every day in Collie, at any time of the day or night, we could hear steam trains trying to move a load of coal, starting off with a slow 'chuff, chuff' and then a racing 'chuff, chuff, chuff', and then slowing down again, trying to get a grip on the railway lines with their big steel wheels. They would pour sand from little things in front of the wheels so they could get a better grip on the line. There was so much weight on the train with the carriages full of coal, it was hard for them to get going sometimes. And we'd hear them whistle when they were going over the two crossings in the township. Everyone had to be aware of the crossing because there were no boom-gates or lights, so we had to get across quickly if there was a train bearing down. We would always try to race the train on our bikes – but we didn't really want to put ourselves in danger, even as children.

"At regular intervals during the day, the time would be signalled from the power station's steam whistle, so we had the eight o'clock, one o'clock and 3 o'clock whistles, so the whole town would know what time it was. This would tell the miners it was time to be on the bus to get to various mines for changes of shift. The coal-fired power station and the Co-Op mine were almost in the town.

"We could smell the steam of the trains. At one stage in my teenage years, I ran across the railway line where hot ashes had been dropped from a train and burnt my foot. It seemed normal practice to just let the hot ash out as they cleared it from the engine."

A typical coal mine entrance
Collie's Griffin Mine entrance, 21-6-27. (Ref: slwa_b3507692_1)

Collie town mural honouring past coal miners

Fires

In winter, Collie is usually freezing, foggy and frosty and subject to floods. On the other extreme, throughout summer, the threat of fire is ever-present.

"Often during school, on a hot, lazy, long day, in between knocking out blow flies with the edge of a ruler – it was just something to do, with a bit of a challenge – we'd get the smell of controlled burns from the surrounding bush wafting through the school windows, as the whole town was surrounded by state forest. So, when I smell bush fires burning now, it takes me back to those days. There were often bush fires out of control, so the fire brigade had a strong presence. And the summer air was often punctuated by the siren – which is a different sound to the mines' whistles, more like an air-raid siren, alerting the volunteer firemen to get to the station for an emergency."

Chapter Nine

Self-Sufficiency

Henry did everything creative and necessary outside the house and Jessie did everything creative and necessary inside. Henry's combined agricultural training, work experience, and general life experience were manifested as he continually improved the house and its facilities, while maximising the productive use of their land and gardens. He also knew how to create or find and deal with food sources outside the house and outside the Collie boundary.

Henry working the home garden plots
Collie, early 1960s

Tomatoes

As Geoff remembers, "The garden produced most of what we ate. The smell of tomato bushes on a very hot day, and eating their rich, red, juicy produce was magnificent!"

However, Robyn also remembers that a little later in life, "Henry put his own blood on the tomatoes because he had haemochromotosis." (This is a medical condition in which a person accumulates too much iron in their blood.) "He had to go to the doctor's every week to get a pint of blood drawn to manage the condition. Henry knew that blood and bone provided excellent nutrients for plants, so he always took his blood home with him, and put it on the vegie patch, the tomatoes in particular."

Unlike Geoff, Robyn says, "I thought it was creepy and refused to eat the tomatoes." Henry's blood was organic, of course, like almost everything else he always used in his garden and for his animals, and nothing went to waste." Everything had a purpose and was used as economically as possible. Vegetable food scraps fed the chickens and chicken manure fed the garden.

Geoff adds with a chuckle, "No poisons were ever used in the garden. But our next- door neighbour had a very annoying rooster that crowed very early every day, waking up the whole neighbourhood. When it came over our fence to harass our chooks, we chased and caught it. Henry injected caponising pellets, a kind of female hormone, under the skin of its leg. The effect was a rooster with a much more delicate 'cock-a-doodle-doo' … and it lost its desire to get in with our chooks."

Bee-Keeping

"In the late 50s, Henry started bee-keeping. He had about forty hives set in various locations, even as far away as Greenbushes where there were a lot of fruit tree orchards, as well as native flowers and flowering timber trees. The nectars from different plants, combined with climate variations, produce different flavoured honey. Different weather in different areas affects plant and bee activity too. I often went out to check the hives and collect honey with my father in his Holden ute with a trailer attached. We used an old farmhouse to harvest the honey. The extractor was like a '44-gallon drum' with a spinning device, with a winding handle at the top. This was very labour intensive and took hours. People from all over Collie came to buy it. We weighed the honey and sold it for 2/6d a pound."

At home, thick layers of honey spread on lavishly buttered fresh bread bought from Booth's Bakery down the road delighted Fisher tastebuds with a sense of utter joy. Geoff's strong interest in the exacting, delicate science of bee-keeping and its sweet rewards were to be created again later in life.

Rabbits

For pocket money, Geoff was able to sell some of their garden produce. "I sold parsley and mint for 1/6d a bunch to Bob Pike, the butcher who as we discovered later, was a silent partner in Dad's honey business.

"When I was ten, I decided to trap rabbits and I did it until I was twelve years old. I found about five traps in the back shed and rode out to the bush to set the traps around well used burrows during late afternoons. Then, to get up very early to check the traps, I had to set my 'Big Ben' alarm clock.

The bell on it was so loud it shook the whole neighbourhood – in fact the whole town – so it was a very stressful way to wake from a dead sleep! I powered up the hill in the morning in darkness, riding my mother's bike because it had an old dynamo with lights. It was often bitterly cold, so I rugged up, but I was used to it. When I got to the rabbits, I had to quickly bang them on the head with a big stick to put them out of their misery. I didn't like doing it, but I was driven by the desire to make pocket money. I sold them to anyone who would pay 2/6d for each one, often to Bob Pike the butcher (along with mint or parsley for 1/6d), and often to Joe Turley. Joe wanted to check their livers for white spots, which showed if they had myxomotosis."

Myxomotosis is a disease caused by Myxomo Virus, introduced to wild rabbits by the Australian government in the 1950s to reduce their devastating numbers.

"When I reached home, I gutted and skinned them in the back yard, but I always left the livers in Joe's rabbits for him to check. Then I'd stake out the skins on the back fence to dry. Later I'd sew them up to make mittens for myself. I knew how to sew them because I had watched my mother. Once I also trapped a big bungarra. It scared the hell out of me, but I released the trap to see it disappear down a rabbit hole. That was pretty exciting!"

A bungarra, Aboriginal for Australia's largest lizard, is commonly known as a 'race-horse goanna', due to its speed.

"Apart from rabbits, we used to have to chop chooks' heads off, then pluck the feathers and gut them using hot water over a bucket. This was a chore expected of us. We didn't enjoy it – we just had to do it, but we had a laugh one day when we saw a headless chook running around the garden! I could hypnotize chickens for a short time too, by stroking them down from their combs, over their beaks, and towards the ground."

And a life filled with pets

Geoff and Robyn with pet white rabbit
Collie 1958

"We had a white fluffy rabbit, but after proving itself to be scared of absolutely everything, and got away too many times, the last time we just let it go and didn't try to find it again. We had a goat for a while too. We milked it every day, but it got out one time too many and ate Joe Turley's vegie patch. Joe lived just up the hill, and he wasn't very happy. I don't remember if we ate the goat, or gave it away – we probably gave it away. We had a 'budgie' for a while, but somehow it got away too. Originally, as a young child, I thought it was called a 'budgeriguard'. I cared about all of our animals, especially the cats. We had three or four cats over time.

Having a cat on my bed was the best thing, especially on a cold winter's night.

"Alan also had a chestnut horse with a white patch on its forehead that he rode and cared for. It was stabled in our back shed. I remember riding it with Alan, sitting behind him, when the girth worked loose and we tipped over, as in slow motion, falling onto the side of a gravel backroad out of town. And once we all came home to find that Alan, at about sixteen years old, had parked a horse-drawn hearse under the mulberry tree up the back yard. It had four wheels with front wheels that turned with the horse. It was an amazing thing – we don't know where he got it. The 'hearse' did not remain there for long, because at the time it seemed a bit spooky."

Alan with his chestnut horse, age 15
Ogden St, Collie

Chapter Ten

Fisher food

Most people used wood-fired Aga and Metter's stoves in the 1950s before gas or electric stoves became common. Some survived through the 1960s, and even into the 1970s, largely because of their reliable baking function. They had to be 'fired-up' daily with wood or coal and needed to be kept alight all day, so chopping wood and stoking the fire until bedtime was a common childhood chore.

Many children had to help their parents around the home in many different ways, and in so doing, learned a diverse range of practical skills with simple science involved, as Geoff did.

"In the kitchen, we had a green Metters stove that we put wood and coal in for the fire. We were always stoking up the coal, and in the mornings, emptying the ashes. It had to be fired up daily and kept burning all day. It provided heat for cooking, but it also provided hot water for the kitchen and bathroom, having water pipes connected to it. No fire meant no dishwashing or hot baths. The stove was kept burning until we went to bed at night. There was a steam pressure-release opening above the shed-laundry for safety, in case someone became over-zealous making the fire. It belched steam and spat water every time we over-heated it. There were no convenient electric or gas hot water systems attached to our house, or many other houses, in these earlier times."

When pressure cookers came into vogue, modernizing Australian kitchens in the late 50s, Jessie boldly invested in one, and her family was amazed by what further culinary delights she could create. Kitchen appliances were evolving and Geoff could see the benefits. Around this time, products like Rice-A-Riso, an instant flavoured form of rice, came onto the market, and it added a bit of modern flair to the Fishers' cuisine. This alternative was more acceptable, because as Geoff says, "Previously, it was often hard to see the individual grains of rice, as they were usually all stuck together, so we called it 'love rice!'"

Nevertheless, the whole family thought Jessie was a fine, capable cook the rest of the time. Henry – sometimes with Geoff's contributions – supplied fresh produce, so Jessie could in turn supply wholesome daily meals, counterbalanced with regular sweet treats for them all. The family usually started their day with hearty bacon and eggs. And for dinner, as was popular everywhere at that time, Jessie frequently cooked affordable tripe, liver or other offal, only some of which Geoff savoured. "What my mother could do with tripe and other entrails was nobody's business!"

At other times Jessie cooked a fresh wild rabbit, or made kangaroo tail soup. Sometimes dinner was a chicken, and sometimes a duck that Henry or Geoff had shot and plucked in the backyard. Jessie could cook many excellent dishes using the cheapest cuts of meat. A favourite snack for all the Fishers involved extra big, thick slices of yeasty bread, smothered generously in thick layers of meat fat called 'dripping'. Every home in the 1950s savoured delicious dripping left over from Sunday roasts.

Jessie was also a dedicated preserver of jams and pickler of all kinds of food, prepared in the wash-house and stored under the house, providing a year-round supply. Food preservation included eggs, also stored under the house. Robyn recalls, "Jessie coated them with something, possibly egg white, to seal the shell, so that in winter when the chickens were not laying, the family always had 'fresh' eggs."

Combining their skills, the Fishers were largely self-reliant and creative when it came to food. Naturally, trips to the local shops, such as the very popular Booth's Bakery just a hundred metres down the road, Bob Pike's butcher shop, and the Co-Op store were needed to supplement supplies.

In the 1950s and early 1960s, the range of commercial confectionary available was very limited, so families usually had 'sweets' or 'desserts' after dinner, and shop-bought sweet things required extra coins to spare. So, in the Fisher family home, frequently at lunchtime, Henry provided fresh, crisp lettuce leaves to be loaded with tablespoons of sugar, rolled up and munched in a flash, ready for the next sweet round. Jessie also made apple fritters, liberally covered in lemon and sugar. However, as Jessie was an excellent cake baker, she regularly made lamingtons, sponges and other cake treats, amongst a wide range of desserts. Her recipes have passed down to Janis and Robyn, in particular her multi-coloured jelly used for indulgent trifle, and rich fruit, carrot and pumpkin recipes. The impact of her baking legacy cannot be underestimated. Cartons of carnation milk and ice-cream were always on hand too.

Whatever the 'sweets', Geoff and Robyn have always been eager for a serve or two – or more – or even forgetting about serves entirely! To some onlookers, they have always demonstrated amazing digestive function, only occasionally making themselves feel ill.

Growing up, plenty of sweet treats were provided for the children's birthday parties, which Jessie arranged for all of her children with equal enthusiasm. However, teenager-Geoff, who relished Jessie's party food and drink treats, did not enjoy the other paraphernalia. "It was very embarrassing with my friends, especially with boys – and all the party hats and kiddies' things."

Head of the table, Geoffrey turning 4 - wearing his party hat! Collie 1951
(L) Alan & Nell Rossiter, (R) Jessie, (C) Janis and friends

Geoffrey (alias Huck Finn!) 4 years old, Collie

Geoffrey, 5 years old, Collie 1952

The Co-Op Store

The Miners' Co-Op store, a delightful destination for the Fishers, provided cheaper products for workers' families. Without a hint of hesitation, both Geoff and Robyn, and no doubt Janice too, still enthusiastically declare their Co-Op store account number – '147!' It seems deeply imprinted in their consciousness, never to be forgotten. As children, it was the most important number in the universe!

Geoff recalls, "Groceries, as well as big bags of chook food were bought, put on the account, and paid for every month. We all took turns to shop, including Henry. The Co-Op was about one kilometre away, so we rode our bikes with Jessie's string bag on the handlebars, or we walked. We put everything on the account, saying 'Just charge it to 147.'"

Robyn also recalls, "When Henry went there, he would always get a packet of Brazil nuts and eat them all, putting the empty packet in his pocket before he reached the check-out! I don't think he was the only one who did it."

Henry also had a sweet tooth equal to his children's. According to Robyn, "He often shopped at the Coles Variety Store in Forrest Street in town, memorable for its red and white striped paper bags. He would get a bag filled with his favourite lollies, chocolate-coated Licorice-Aniseed Rings, or sometimes Humbugs. Having devoured some of them privately on his way home, he then hid the rest high in the broom cupboard on a special shelf that was 'his shelf'. A red and white striped paper bag could usually be seen up there. Lollies were just a normal part of life at home. Although Jessie loved baking cakes, and making sweets, she didn't eat them as often, preferring savoury things."

Henry, Jessie, Geoff, Janis and Robyn at country fair 1950s
– about to buy fairy floss?

Chapter Eleven

Swimming: Part one

Geoff's earliest memory of swimming was of being at the Kalgoorlie public swimming pool in summer when he was three years old.

"My parents took me there and I remember holding onto the side of the pool, feeling excited by this new experience. Even though I couldn't swim yet, I was not afraid. I felt happy and secure. When I was five or six years old, my father took me to the Collie River by the swing bridge. He was trying to teach me to swim, but that was difficult, because he was holding me in the water. With a lot of repeated effort later on, from six to nine years old, I learned to swim by myself. I studied pictures in the Pix and Post magazines with photos of Olympian long-distance swimmers, trying to get the same arm style, especially for the Australian Crawl. I usually practised in the Collie River with my friends, Jock Gillard, Warwick Randall, David Palmer and his little brother, Graham.

"Growing up, the Collie River was the most wonderful playground for kids like me and my friends. We'd go down to the river and we'd walk through mud and quicksand, which we likened to all the Tarzan movies we had seen, and we were always swimming through reeds and swampy areas. One girl swimming with us, Gail Baker, claimed I saved her life in the river when she thought she was drowning. She couldn't breathe through her leaking face mask, and was sure she was going to die. She was struggling at the time, so I came to her rescue. We were all diving with face masks in a particularly reedy part, between the swingy bridge and the Co-Op Bridge.

"There were certain areas of the river that had a lot of fish, like Perch, for us to see. And I liked diving down to the bottom of the river trying to find things. I remember impressing a girl, Merilyn Little, and her sister Valerie, by surfacing with discarded kitchen things like a tea strainer and spoon and other little treasures. That was the day I also slipped and fell onto some old jetty boards, sending shock waves through my nether regions. Huge embarrassment followed, and a hasty retreat.

"On hot, lazy summer days, greenish-blue shimmering dragonflies hovered around us. We used to get leeches on our legs too. We'd take them off and turn them inside out on sticks and put them on an ants' nest or in a fire. We always had a fire going to keep warm on colder days. We also had another favourite swimming spot called the 'blue pool' which was a bit scary because it was so deep. It was an abandoned open cut mine filled with water. And there was another very favourite place near the middle of town, where all the swamps were. We caught tadpoles for hours, and played 'Tarzan' games there. Sadly, the swamps were later excavated to let the river run freely to prevent winter flooding.

"Once, when I was about ten, I went down to the river near the Soldiers' Memorial Park next to the trotting track in the middle of town. I caught a perch with a bent pin tied to cotton. Then I felt sorry for it. I was holding it in the water so it wouldn't die, and it got away, ha ha! I thought it was amazing that I could catch a fish with a bent pin. All the kids had areas that were special like this, and another one was the 'swing bridge' (a suspension bridge), which we called 'the swingy', very close to where we lived. We got on it together and made it swing as hard as we could.

"Near Christmas, I used to get up in our mulberry tree with David Palmer, both in our bathers, and we'd have a feed of mulberries – which were delicious when they were really ripe – big, juicy, black mulberries – and we'd paint ourselves from head to toe with the purple juice and then ride downtown, or to the swingy, or we'd go from the swingy further up to our most favourite spot called 'the logs' and we'd jump in to wash it off, creating a purple patch around us.

"One of the most disappointing times of my young life was the time of a summer flood. While climbing a fence, I stood on half a broken cup and cut my heel. It was bandaged up to protect it from infection, but at this time the river was a raging torrent flowing under the swingy bridge, and I couldn't go in to enjoy it. That was my worst memory of childhood! – even worse than when I ruptured my spleen and broke four bones in my left foot.

"Our high school swimming races were held at Minninup, a bend in the river just out of town. There was an equivalent distance of a 55-yard pool set up there. We had to swim to the other side of the river, line up, and race back. I was so excited catching up in a race, but near the finish, I took in a mouthful of water and choked on it, coming in a disappointing second."

Swimming: Part two

A splenic affair

"One summer, when I was about fifteen, I rode my bike a little bit further out of town to a part of the river called Telfers — it was just a swimming spot with that name, maybe from a farm around there. It had a swing built on a tall framework. We had a metal bar that we could hang onto with both hands to swing out and dive in. The embankment was packed with logs to stop it eroding. I was enjoying myself and, in retrospect, must have been trying to impress a couple of girls. I swung out and turned around to dive as I was coming back in, which is all-well-and-good if you get your timing right, but I left it too late, and dived straight onto some big logs and knocked myself out. I was falling backwards into the water when a local school teacher witnessed the event, dragged me out, and took me home.

"I was probably concussed, but I just went inside. As always, if I had a problem, I would just sleep it off, so I put myself to bed in the back verandah sleepout. But I couldn't sleep and I was still seeing spots. Things weren't going too well. Nobody was home. My father was at work in the mines and he wasn't going to be home from the afternoon shift until 11 o'clock that night. My mother must have been out shopping on her bike, because she hadn't learned to drive.

"When I realized that I wasn't right, I went into the lounge room and got onto our old black Bakelite phone. I had to wind its handle around a few times, and then the exchange-operator answered. We knew operators would sometimes listen in to calls, and they knew everything that was going on in town.

I said, 'I need a doctor.'

Then she asked, 'What's the problem?'

And I said, 'Oh, I don't know, I'm not well, I've hurt myself.'

Bakelite wind-handle phone, connecting to phone operator

"Soon a doctor turned up to check me out. Then he rushed off leaving me alone a few minutes longer. He returned driving an ambulance, but had to flag down a passer-by to manage a stretcher and help put me in the ambulance. At the hospital, x-rays showed a ruptured spleen. So, they put me in the ambulance again, with a lovely nurse this time, and drove me to Fremantle Hospital, three hours away. Later, as I was bleeding internally, my mother was waiting for my father to come home from the mine so he could give permission for the surgeon to operate – she couldn't give permission because she was just a woman!"

Geoff had to have a 'splenectomy' to remove his damaged, haemorrhaging spleen tissue. An injured spleen bleeds internally, which can lead to death, so it had to be taken out. It was thought he had a tiny bit left, but a major event later in life required scans that do not support this.

"After hospital, I had to recover for about another week in a lovely convalescent home, the Lady Lawley Cottage-by-the-Sea, set along the beach on Marine Parade in Cottesloe. Back home I did my best to recover, but just being a kid, one day I was wrestling with David Palmer. I tried to throw him over my head by falling down backwards, lifting him over the top. The only trouble was, he tried to save himself and he fell on my left foot, breaking four bones, which went like a machine gun, like 'brrr-brrr-brrr', in rapid succession. But I still rode my bike home.

"As usual, after such 'an event', I tried to sleep it off. I thought, 'It'll come good', but it didn't. It just ached and ached, so I had to tell my parents … so off to the Collie hospital for x-rays and a plaster cast. My father's comment was, 'Well, that'll probably do him good. It'll slow him down!' Soon I was going to school on crutches with George Stewart from across the road, who dropped me off on his way to his Dry-Cleaning business. My foot ached like hell whenever I put it on the ground on those cold Collie mornings.

"Collie sometimes has huge floods and all the shops would get inundated, the Co-Op and the hardware store and the others, so they cleaned out the river with bulldozers, and a lot of those beautiful spots that we spent our childhood in, disappeared overnight. There had been lots of beautiful weeping willows with all their leaves drooping down to the water."

Chapter Twelve

Bikes

Geoff's passion for bikes started very early in life. It started with the very exciting three-wheeler when he was about three years old. He was able to ride down Ogden Street to his little heart's content, with plenty of space and little or no traffic to worry about in those days. Soon he could balance and ride on just two wheels. Naturally, by the time he was nine, he dreamt of riding 'a proper bike'.

However, in his ninth year, on Christmas Day in 1956, he was shocked by his special Christmas gift, left nicely wrapped and placed under the Christmas tree in the back verandah sleepout. As he picked the long, heavy parcel up, ripping off the paper wrapping, he realised he'd been tricked and thought, 'How could this be happening?'

"I found it was a 4 inch by 2 inch (commonly pronounced '4B2') piece of jarrah timber. Bitterly disappointed and full of anger, I threw it as far as I could up the back yard! Soon Henry and Jessie coaxed me back inside where I found a handsome 'proper bike' waiting for me. I just about exploded with excitement and was out on the road as soon as …

"It was in blue tones and traditional – not one of those high risers. I can only imagine how pleased and proud my parents were then, but I was too self-absorbed to notice.

"In 1957, when I was ten, my favourite place at home was

the back shed, where I disassembled and re-assembled an old Malvern Star racing bike. I would take it down to the last ball-bearing. I had discovered professional road racing".

He promptly painted it red with enamel paint to make it 'go faster'.

"Every week, I prepared this way for my next bike race. A school friend's dad, Charlie Barron, used to help his sons fix their bikes – I watched and learned a lot from him.

"I would disassemble everything, wash everything in kerosene, pack the ball-bearings in grease, and reassemble. Before race day, I'd select a gear for the day because I didn't have the luxury of a set of gears."

Geoff, age 11, with prized Malvern Star Pro-racing bike, 1958

"I was a professional juvenile bike rider. Sunday morning was race day in Collie. These were professional bike races. Everyone put money in to go in a race and they'd divvy up the prize money out of that money pool. So, we could win a race and get £1.2.6d (1 pound 2 shillings and 6 pence), or we could come second and get 15 shillings or come third and get 5 shillings and 6 pence.

"As it was a professional sport, even kids had to pay to race. It was usual in winter to have handicapped races. For summer, the town built a bitumen cycling velodrome right next to the football oval in the centre of town. For velodrome races, we had to strip the bikes down to the bare essentials; no brakes or gears. We raced with a 'fixed wheel with no ratchet', so that we would slow down using our legs and feet, pushing back to brake. This meant every foot movement controlled the bike and we couldn't glide. We had to stiffen our legs to slow the bike down or stop. Sudden stops would have caused crashes. We couldn't just free-wheel – my feet would keep going around and around – that's called riding with a 'fixed wheel' or 'fixie'.

"When I was road racing in winter, I would have to choose a gear suitable for that race on the day, as I couldn't afford a bike with gears. I had a number of different chain gear wheels and sprockets and a chart to help me choose the best combination for the race conditions of the day. If I chose a gear wheel and sprocket that was too highly geared for me, with my skinny little legs, I couldn't handle it. In that case, the number of revolutions would be too slow, too hard going up a hill, but going down would be great! I would have a free-wheeling ratchet on, so that I could coast down the hills and give my legs a rest, like they do in the Tour de France.

"One highlight was winning a road race, although Dennis

Barron claimed I cut him off in the sprint, which could have been true because I was battling to go fast, to keep up. I had skinny, little legs, not very powerful. Anyway, I won a silver ashtray with a little medallion that spun around, with 'Fallen Riders Memorial 1957' on it because people had died in a road race, years earlier.

"Some of the Collie riders were well known for getting into 'fisty-cuffs' while racing. They'd get angry with each other for not taking a turn in front, bearing in mind that in Collie in those days, a difference of opinion meant punching someone's lights out! They didn't resolve things by talking. That seemed to be the mentality of many coal miners and their children.

"On many lazy afternoons, the Bury kids and I entertained ourselves with an old motorbike frame complete with brakes but no engine. We'd push it to the top of the laneway behind our house to race it downhill, negotiating a right-angled left turn, hoping for the best, but sometimes crashing into the neighbour's old wooden dunny."

Chapter Thirteen

My primary school years

"I went to Amaroo Primary School in Collie. 'Amaroo' is an Aboriginal word meaning 'place of water'. School was interesting – lots of things happened there. I liked my school uniform which was much like a security blanket. I usually rode or walked to school. As Collie has some freezing winter temperatures, if I was riding my bike, I had to pull my jumper down over my hands in chilly winds. Riding 'no-hands' helped develop my sense of balance. I clearly remember walking to school in winter, in fog, on very cold mornings. The classrooms had wood fires in winter because it got so cold, but there was no such thing as a gas or electric heater or air conditioner back then."

In winter, Collie can have temperatures as low as minus 1 or 2 degrees, often recording the coldest temperatures in the State.

"At school and at home, hoses would snap, being full of ice. And at home, I especially liked seeing the ducks' pond with iced-over water, because I enjoyed breaking the ice up to let the ducks have a drink. It was the same with the chooks' water. Later, the frosty fog would lift and the sun would shine on a beautiful fresh day.

"Whatever the weather, the journey walking home from school was about one kilometre. The highlight of the walk was passing Mrs Cherry's lunch and lolly shop, particularly when I could buy a Choo-Choo bar, arriving home with a black tongue."

Choo-Choo bars were very popular, being a deep purplish-black colour with a liquorice-aniseed flavour. They lasted a very long time, up to half a day or so (for some people), and were considered excellent value, costing only threepence (3d).

Geoff found travelling to and from school was usually pleasurable, but school itself was a challenge:

"The primary school headmaster was a faceless person, just a figurehead of power. I would occasionally have been sent to him for 'the cuts', but I can't remember that exactly."

In spite of the headmaster, Geoff liked most of his class teachers, although he remembers, "One male teacher, Mr Wright, who had polio in one leg, was quite understanding, except for the fateful day when the pronunciation of 'France' was in question. It was instantly a battle of wills. This was in Grade 7. We were being taught how to say 'France' and he told me it was 'Fraa..h..nce' and I said 'France', like 'pants', and he said 'Fraa..h..nce' again and I again said 'France', like 'pants', and then he hit me on the fingers with a ruler."

Music

One of Geoff's better primary school memories involved his regular duty to choose and play long-playing-records (known as LPs), providing brass band music for all the kids to march into class. He would play traditional brass band music which was generally supplied to schools by the Education Department.

"I had shown an interest, so I was commandeered for the task. There were a few tracks that were my favourites, including classical pieces that were not just the usual marching tunes. There were some beautiful pieces. *Under The Double Eagle* and *Colonel Bogey* were two brass band marching favourites.

No doubt, in order to break any sense of predictability and his own boredom, Geoff managed to entertain himself.

"I sometimes played them at the wrong, slow speed, making them sound deep and dragging, and then I would speed them up, then slow them right down again. That amused me no-end! I don't think it amused the staff as much as the students. I loved having access to all of the switches and I was intrigued by how to manage the old sound system. For further interest, as the children were marching up and down the stairs, I would turn individual classroom's speakers on, so the music would suddenly come on in the rooms they were walking past."

This would have seemed mysterious, leading to some amused students if they could work out what was happening. One could suppose that the staff secretly enjoyed his antics too, as they allowed him to keep his special music duties.

Playing the brass band LPs subsequently inspired Geoff to learn to play the cornet with the Collie Brass Band from 1958, when he was ten.

"As the youngest member, I had to have a uniform cut down to my size. Band members taught me to play the cornet, and I also had extra lessons with somebody from that band. I had to learn the notes, and the fingering for each note. They gave me things like 'F-A-C-E' patterns, or 'Every Dog Deserves A...' something or other, to help me remember where the notes were, to get familiar. I had to learn whether the notes were below or above the staff, a bit confusing at first. It's not easy to quickly take up new stuff like that and

I'm sure our close neighbours struggled for a while too."

11-year-old Geoff with cornet, in cut down to size band uniform, 1958

"I loved the music so much that sometimes I'd drift off in the middle of a piece when we were practising. I would be swept up in it, lost in the drama of the brass band sounds. I'd completely lose my place in the music. We marched around the streets playing for the general public on Sundays and for special community events. We practised a couple of nights a week in a hall and sometimes while marching around town. I'm sure my parents would have watched us playing, if it wasn't a Sunday when my father was working. The band was just part of the town community, so when there was an event on, people would line the streets and cars would stop at intersections to watch and listen as we passed by.

"There was an old guy, Jim Fease, playing his bass drum, with Jim Old playing cornet, and Jim Noonan playing euphonium. Jim was a very common English/Scottish name, usually pronounced 'Jemmy' or 'Jummy', and many brought the brass band tradition to Australia with them. The band taught me a lot.

"Once, I was riding across town to brass band practice with my cornet in a leather cornet case hanging off the handlebars of my mother's bike with the lights. I thought I'd see how far I could ride without looking but I crashed into the back of a car, which snapped me out of that idea. I felt a bit silly, but I managed to continue on. No damage, not to the car, the bike or the cornet, and I must have been going slowly enough not to kill myself!

"My legacy, passed on from my maternal grandfather, Arthur William Mardon, seems to be his deep involvement in music. Although he was a PMG (Post Master General) phone technician, he was also a dedicated brass band player.

"Arthur took a lot of pride in his musical accomplishments. In 1911, at twenty-two years of age, he married my grandmother, Daisy, who was nineteen. They both lived in Cue in the Goldfields then. When I was born in 1947, Arthur played in brass bands in Kalgoorlie and around the Goldfields. Before that, he played in other bands in other places and later, around 1930, he was a bandmaster in a brass band in South Australia – his birthplace."

Grandfather, Arthur Mardon, in PMG technician uniform

"Arthur had previously played in the famous Newcastle Steelworks Brass Band in New South Wales, where he had also lived. I think he played the bass, euphonium and trombone. He went with this band to countless competitions and they won every competition in Australia in which they took part. He went with the Newcastle Steelworks Band on tour for a year between 1924 and 1925 to compete in the British Empire Exhibition and British championship titles which involved bands from Australia, India, South Africa, Canada and Britain. The band won a lot of prize money and medals and, being the overall winners, had the great honour of performing for King George V at the Exhibition."

The band's competition prize money ranged from hundreds of British pounds to four thousand pounds, a huge sum of money in the 1920s. The Mardon family has copies of Arthur's travel photos, and news articles praising their talent with pictures of their awards, all printed in Great Britain and Australia following the band's huge success. A book has been written about the Newcastle Steelworks Band, entitled *A Musical Mission of Empire* by Jack Greaves. The honoured band was invited to record several LPs with RCO Records in the Aeolian Hall, London, in 1924. These recordings can still be heard on YouTube.

Arthur Mardon, seated front/far right with his double bass at Bristol championship 1924, leading up to final win at British Empire Exhibition 1925

While Arthur Mardon was in England, he met another woman, Lavinia Hall. She had his son in 1925, after he returned with his band to Australia. The son was named Arthur Mardon Hall. He died in 1986, apparently knowing little about his father, except that Arthur had played in a famous brass band, and that he was from Australia where he already had a family. Compromising family matters such as these, often considered too shameful, were rarely discussed, merely left to secret rumour. Initially, Arthur returned to South Australia, but moved to Kalgoorlie/Boulder in 1932, and finally to Northbridge in Perth where he died in 1951.

Young Arthur Mardon, centre back, working as porter at train station, location unknown
(*Note the likeness between young Arthur and Geoff.)

Music coursed its way through the Fisher-Mardon clan veins. When Geoff was eight or nine, his father bought him a banjo, recognizing his interest in music, and paid for lessons, "… but I just didn't take to it. Then I learned to play the cornet in the Collie Brass Band."

Although Geoff has never been a singer, he has always enjoyed listening to talented and accomplished singers.

"I remember as a child in my school holidays, sometimes visiting my Aunty Thelma and Uncle Joe, Henry's brother, in their Clydesdale Street home in Como, on their standard half-acre block. Aunty Thelma could sing beautifully. She had a lovely singing voice, and she played the piano. In her day, she played piano in theatres to accompany silent movies."

Entertainment

On the home front, apart from singing or the playing of musical instruments, records and radio were the main sources of listening entertainment before TV arrived.

"I have fond memories of lying on my stomach on the floor of the lounge room, watching the red light at the bottom of the radiogram, fascinated, listening to my favourite shows such as *Davy Crocket*. Also, *Night Beat with Randy Stone*, which was a detective serial and gave me the first sex scene I ever heard. It involved a man, and a woman who said, 'Oh, darling, I'm so cold!' and he said, 'I'll keep you warm …' I loved listening to *Davy Crocket* and *The Lone Ranger*."

Dad 'n Dave, an Aussie comic program, and *Blue Hills*, were other radio serials that he followed with delight, like so many young and old Australians in those years. Geoff enjoyed these home entertainments, but rarely to the exclusion of more active pursuits.

"Paddy Turley, who was older than me and my friends, would turn up in Ogden Street dressed as a cowboy threatening to kill us all – he scared the crap out of us! – except when he had a broken leg, and we could get away because he couldn't keep up with us. We played 'cowboys and Indians' a lot."

Thanks to the bell!

At school, it was a joyful day when Geoff managed to get 'bell-ringing duty'. At that time, all schools had a school bell set on a tall frame and rung by pulling on a long rope attached to the bell. It was usually set just outside the main building, by the playground. Ringing the bell announced the start and end of classes, assembly times, lunch and break times.

"Being the bell monitor, I had to remember what time it was. I would run down the corridors, down the stairs and across the bitumen yard to the bell, giving it a good old ring. Then I'd start getting a bit creative with the bell-ringing. I'd never just do the same bell-ring every day."

Most activities in the classroom were often rather too slow and hum-drum for boys like Geoff. He recalls, "In class time, making the whole class laugh was the entertainment for the day ... so how could they dislike me? Besides, there's no choice about that sort of thing, if you just do it all the time. It's not as if you choose to be like that, you just are. On the other hand, every stage of school was just a bridge to the next stage. There was no graduation, no highlight for me. Oh, I was glad to go on to the next thing alright, thinking, 'Well, I just suffered through that, now onto the next thing, with a new set of pencils, a new set of books, put covers on them, write your name on, now run around the oval until you're totally exhausted and go to sleep in class – what else was there?"

Fortunately, school provided the company of many females, and Geoff enjoyed them all. "I especially loved all of the young female teacher graduates and had crushes on many of them. Folk dancing gave me the chance to meet and dance with all those female teachers and the girls. It was all those beautiful legs and short skirts – I couldn't get enough of them! But at one of the special school events, I was feeling 'really off'. While marching into school, I vomited in the hallway. That was supremely embarrassing. Staff had to come and clean it up because I was so sick and couldn't do it myself.

"There were not many big events at school, like fetes, but sometimes different entertainers visited. For example, there were people who trained dogs dressed up in cutesy clothes that danced and did tricks, or magicians, or a ventriloquist with 'that ugly doll' that clacked with a wooden mouth.

"More interesting were the visits involving a 16mm projector with pictures of wildlife – which we take for granted nowadays, being able to watch documentaries on TV and YouTube. We had to sit still and wait while the projector was set up and the film was carefully threaded on, and then it would break down, and they'd have to start again. The single, little speaker in each classroom providing the sound for the film was usually crackly and weak too."

Geoff tried a variety of sports in primary school. "I tried playing football, but found myself being blinded by the sunlight when out on the oval. I was unable to keep my eyes open, possibly due to an undiagnosed temporary eye condition. This made it impossible for me to play at the time, but ultimately, I wasn't very good at football, not physically equipped for it in some way, so let it go. I also competed in running events. I tried as hard as I could, but found that, although I could run fast, there was always someone faster. I often came second or third or fourth, but didn't win prizes – and not for lack of trying. I was often beaten by Dennis Barron."

Geoff and his sister, Janice, both played tennis with relative success, but moved on to other sports, like hockey. However, for Geoff, swimming and bike riding were constant pleasures.

Sugar and cream

"I was forever going to the dentist, Mr Smith, and I would ride my bike down to appointments. School allowed me to attend dental appointments and I remembered the appointment times in relation to my bell-ringing duties. Mr Smith had a big tummy that rattled and bubbled and made long gurgling sounds, as his stomach was pressed up against my ear. Ah … the leather belts on the drills singing their merry tune, going around and around on pulleys … the drill slowly grinding its way through my teeth … and the sight of that great big stainless steel and glass needle that was so big, it cast a shadow over me as it approached my young sensitive gums."

Geoff had a lot of fillings, probably due to the sugary foods he consumed. He doesn't remember anyone telling him that he shouldn't eat sugary things, although it's something he would most likely have discounted, especially as his family enjoyed the same things.

After World War II, particularly by the 1950s, confectionary availability increased with a changing, stronger economy, and 'better off' parents were able to give their children weekly, fortnightly or monthly 'pocket money', often one or two shillings. Some children chose to spend it on chocolate, lollies, ice-creams and cool drinks. Comics were very popular too. However, many families still struggled financially, and could not give their children any pocket money – so they had to earn money doing jobs in the neighbourhood, or simply 'go without'.

Illicit lollies

Both the Royal Theatre, a cinema in the centre of town, and Gino's, a milk bar with sweets and chips next door, typically provided confectionary for movie-goers and these places hold special memories for Geoff. Together with his friends, David Palmer and his little brother, he sought the perfect combination of sugar and excitement. More than once, they snuck into Gino's back storeroom, having secreted empty flour sacs in their pockets.

"Then, while the owner was busy with customers, we could see there were big barrels of lollies, like Aladdin's Cave, full of treasure. So, while the owner was busy, we would sneak in and madly fill our sacs with lollies, even jelly crystals and Maltesers, then run like the wind down to the river to hide under the Collie Co-Op bridge to eat our fill, stashing the remainder there for another day. One time later, we were shocked to get caught in the act. The owner was so stunned and we were so terrified, we ran for our lives but were not pursued. That was the last time we committed the terrible crime! The next time we went there through the front entrance and we weren't recognised, luckily, but we had already reformed!

"At school, I often managed to become the 'milk monitor' so I could drink all the left-over milk, loving the extra cream on top."

In the 1950s, governments supplied all primary schools, Monday to Friday, with small bottles of milk for all students to drink in the morning, making sure there was adequate nutrition for them to study. Not all students liked drinking plain milk, especially if the weather was warm, affecting the temperature and taste of the milk, curdling the cream on top. There were often some bottles remaining. Geoff had his own strategy: "I used to take sweet strawberry or raspberry flavouring to put in the milk.

"And I remember at home, getting up early, silently exiting the house, negotiating the noisy old door knobs and tip-toeing over creaky floorboards to get out of the house, to drink the cream off the top of the milk which was left in an aluminium pail near the front door. Then I'd be off to wake up my best friend, David Palmer, to go adventuring."

Friends

Geoff's best friends, apart from special action-friends like David Palmer, included some Italian boys.

"I remember one boy's name, Dominic Italiano. And there was another kid who came to school one day who spoke no English. He was put in the back of the class, and he just nodded off to sleep, because he probably couldn't understand anything and was dog-tired … with all the journeys he had made … but he was a lovely guy. There were Polish kids too, like Marian and Caju Cyzka who lived next door. They were good friends and I used to play with them a lot. At school, I didn't find their lunches strange at all, and I'd swap a cheese and salad sandwich for their Polish sausage. I went over to their place a lot to play, especially because they ate different food. I sometimes stole a slurp of carnation milk out of a can in their fridge. Polish people were called 'Polaks' in Australia at that time. Other good friends, who were neighbours too, were Leo and Paddy Turley. Their dad, Joe, bought my rabbits.

"I remember an incident with my neighbours, forever burned in my memory: One early morning I went to the Burys' for breakfast. They had a slow-burning stove called an 'Aga' that stayed hot all day, and in the kitchen, I saw an amazing event. I was shocked to see Mrs Bury sitting on Mr Bury's lap in front of the fire! I'd never seen anything like that before because my parents had never done that in front of me.

"The Bury's eldest son Ivan, much older than his brothers

and me, had a fully chromed racing bike which impressed me. AND he could balance, perfectly stationary, on the steepest part of the velodrome! This was important in a match race.

"However, when we were nine, the younger Bury boys seemed to turn on me and decided to hang me by the neck in their cubby house. I feared for my life that day but luckily escaped!

"As for girls, at times I played with Roddy Dransfield, a neighbour three doors away. We liked to hide and pretend to leave home forever, taking some hessian bags for comfort and fresh apples for food, but by dinner time we'd always get hungry and decide to give up and go home. Then there was a girl called Maureen who seemed to have a very difficult life at home. One time, I sent her a birthday card, which she said at a reunion forty years later, was a turning point in her life because nobody had ever done that for her before. She thought it was an amazing, thoughtful gift. I have often reflected on the impact of this.

"As for other girls at school, they were all gorgeous … but they would just come and go, like flowers growing in the wilderness. I especially loved the young female graduate teachers – the highlight of my early education – even just talking to them. I took any chance to be up close and personal with them. I don't know if that was obvious."

Some 'not-friends'

"At primary school, we were all terrorised by by the Stone brothers. They were the best fighters, more like the school Mafia. You didn't argue with the Stone brothers, because they were bigger, older, faster. They were a family gang of their own. If you looked at them the wrong way, you could end up with a knuckle sandwich. They were a year or so older. They were 'from the other side of the tracks', so to speak. But they were the best high jumpers. They could do the Western Roll over the high jumps to impossible heights. I didn't have a confrontation with them myself, but there was another shorter guy, Barry Hargreaves, who had a protector, twice our size. I always regretted not punching his lights out for hassling me. I was ready to do it once, in a particular confrontation in the toilets underneath the school. He wanted to hit me, but for some reason didn't – and I didn't lash out because of his big protector standing behind him and the protective gang around them.

"These confrontations were normal in schools and mining towns. Their idea of an argument was to say, 'Come outside!' That was the mentality – it wouldn't matter why. They'd just make things up to have a fight."

Alan

"The most shocking event of my primary school years, at the age of ten, was to be told 'you'd better go home – NOW!' – because my brother Alan had suicided. He was seventeen years and three months old. That was a terrible day. I was just ambling through the school yard at the time, when the deputy principal approached me and suggested that I go home immediately, but he didn't tell me why. I thought that was weird. Then I noticed kids whispering things that I didn't understand. That was very frustrating. I don't know what I was thinking when I got home, but I must have had an idea that something was wrong ... so I walked into the house, down the corridor and out to the back verandah. My mother was sitting there with bloodshot eyes, and Kath Dransfield (my friend Roddy's mother) from two doors down, was sitting with her.

"The wall of the sleepout was covered in blood. It shocked me to the core. Alan had shot himself. I got very tearful. And I got very annoyed with the well-meaning neighbour who said, 'Oh, let him cry, it'll do him good.' That was like a stab to my heart! I just didn't want her to talk about it, especially that way. I can't remember the words spoken to me apart from that.

"The police and ambulance had obviously been and gone, and my father was still at work, and he probably wasn't contactable. I think people came around like they do. And I just remember staying next door that night, on their very clean linen, on a verandah on the other side of their house. I hardly slept. I was emotional and angry.

"After that, I can't remember going back to school although I seem to have some recollection of people talking behind their hands. It would have been pretty big news in primary school for the kids to talk about. But for me, there wasn't any counselling or caring chats with special people. It took me another forty years to overcome the trauma – with counselling sessions as an adult.

"I can't remember seeing or talking to my sister Janice, and I think Robyn was a baby then. I gather Alan had been fired from his job and couldn't face our father. He was seven years older than me and, of course, I had no idea about his issues at the time. He had used a .22 rifle that was kept at home for hunting."

Before this, barely two years old at the time, Robyn vaguely remembers her brother. "I was playing on the floor with some things from out of the cupboard, and I looked up to see him standing in the doorway, maybe with his arms folded, leaning against the door frame – but nothing more."

Alan, age 17 – Collie. 1957

Alan's grave, Collie Cemetery

Chapter Fourteen

My high school years

"The Collie Senior High School uniform consisted of a dark blue jumper with a red and light blue stripe, long pants or shorts, shoes and socks. I cared about my appearance, and always polished my shoes. Brad Loftus, whose parents owned the men's wear store in town, always had the best shirts and trousers … but I thought the uniform made everyone equal. Deputy headmasters always told us that we shouldn't stand about with hands in pockets, but it was often very cold. I had the standard Brylcreem 'comb-over' in a wave parted on the left side, because 'A little dab'll do ya!' I still love the memory of its fragrance."

Brylcreem (spelling used on product) was a popular, slightly greasy men's hair cream that men and boys of all ages used in an attempt to look handsome and cool, like rock & roll singers and movie stars. Everyone knew the entertaining 1960s Brylcreem jingle on TV and radio advertisements, which can still be seen and heard on YouTube.

Geoff adds, "High school was interesting and I loved biology, geography and physics. I was interested in questions asked by our biology teacher, such as, 'If the train is coming into the station, and the train master had just made a cup of coffee, should he put the cream on straight away because he's got to go away for ten minutes, or when he comes back? What are the possible outcomes? … The cream is a thermal layer on top, keeping the coffee hot.

"But I was not a good student. School was so structured that it really didn't suit me. And I asked the wrong questions, it seemed. Whatever intelligence I had didn't fill their criteria, so I didn't think I was intelligent. I could do things and fix almost anything. At the time, I thought I probably had the intelligence best suited to a trade. I struggled a bit with maths and history. And I failed French. I could answer all questions in class, and was enthusiastic, but it often didn't translate into exam success – but I was inconsistent around exam study too. I was often out on a Lambretta scooter with my friend, Keith Dewar. I was easily distracted. I wasn't overly nervous about exams and I would hang in there until the last minute, but would have to make some things up. The girls would always finish first, and knew the answers – that's why I thought I would marry one!

"When I had homework to do, I would study in the kitchen or in a shed up the back yard. The 'shed' was an old corrugated, galvanized tank cut in half, lying on its side. It was used as a wood shed, which I took over to use as a study. I ran a long electric cord to it for lighting and a heater so I could study in there at night. I could also escape my mother's never-ending dancing lessons on the back verandah."

In his first year of high school, still twelve years old, Geoff wrote this letter to Jessie:

24 Ogden St Collie,
9th May 1960.

Dear mum I hope you and the kids are having a good t time, because I'm pretty sure I am, cookin' me own meals.

I had York here Saturday night, and boy was it bun, we had plenty of fun but we still had to do the dishes and so on.

I have been looking after the place, like, et sweepin' the floor, cleanin' the stove with bon-ami and washing the bath with a bit of bon-ami (spelt without looking.) and (mistake) trusol.

Tell "Robin" I can't wait to see her.

I made the double bed and

> the two beds out in the sleepout
> and I am just going to sweep the
> back verandah.
> You can tell everybody that I
> came second in the cycling on Sunday
> but as yet I have not picked up my
> prize money. (here comes dad) I might
> come up with dad (now he's starting to
> sing "Lindy" [Lindys]) when he comes up to
> pick you mob up (I will bring me
> own [cornet]). Anyway I hope you all have a
> good time.
> give my regards to aunty Dot and Uncle
> Harry and the rest.
>
> Au revoir ma dame.
>
> Geoff.
>
> {write back soon.}

Ah, the girls…

"In high school, I spent a lot of time staring at Lorraine, the local Ford dealer's daughter. She was special. Lorraine was always 'just out of reach' and held a major singing role in the school opera *Mikado*. I was in the chorus, and struggling with it all. I didn't really like singing, but I got corralled into it. I helped make up the numbers. But I just loved the music. And I was impressed with the male singing teacher, who was a frustrated opera singer.

"And then there was another girl who suffered occasional epileptic fits, who put me on the spot. One day she asked me in the school quadrangle if we were 'going out'. She was looking at her tiny girl's watch with no sweep-hand, waiting for me to answer, and the seconds were ticking over like years, but after five seconds passed – and I think I got out of that by running off. I can't remember agreeing to anything! But I remember the look on her face as she looked at that watch without the sweep-hand, while counting the seconds.

"In year 12, there was another girl, who I walked home after *Mikado* practice, maybe to do some homework together. Her father was a motorbike racer I admired. But she wanted more than I was ready to give her. She wanted me to kiss her. I remember her particular perfume and when I smell it again, it takes me back in an instant … she was puckering up for 'the kiss' … and in a nervous moment, I took off for home before she opened her eyes again! By year's end, our 'leaving year', she fell pregnant to a classmate and had to leave school to have her baby. School girl pregnancies were all much more difficult in those days, in the mid-1960s, but I believe she and her partner are still together.

"I also hankered after a gorgeous Italian girl who also wore an amazing fragrance that caused a rush of hormones. I remember being with her at the Collie Miner's Institute Hall with a 60s band banging out popular cover songs on stage. The hall was filled with ultraviolet flashing lights that made everyone's clothes simply buzz with a neon effect that set my mind aglow. The music and perfumes in the still, cold air of Collie at night were exciting. I kissed her once, and that memory lingered for many years.

"And I remember another time, walking a girl home to what we called 'White City', a housing development populated with small white painted homes, probably built with asbestos. The town was divided in two by the railway line, so it was understood as a 'them and us' division. They were on the other side of the tracks, on the other side of town from where we lived. I remember talking for hours – it seemed like hours – sitting on the front fence, which was just a low wooden fence with cyclone wire, instead of pickets, and then walking all the way home to the other side of town at one o'clock in the morning. I walked in bright moonlight, with still cold air. I felt a deep sense of satisfaction of an evening well spent. This was the romantic essence of my teenage years.

"And then there was Maureen Fogarty and her little sister, who I often visited because I was 'going with her'. We would sit around for hours in front of a warm fire. After one such visit, I got home and found I had a rip in the crutch of my trousers and thought 'Oh no, it has been obvious the whole evening and nobody told me!' – one of those embarrassing events that are etched in my memory. Her father was a mine manager, a status position in our town. A big outing for us was to see a movie at The Royal Theatre or the Bow Cinema."

Entertainment

Sadly, these two theatres disappeared from Collie when analogue television came onto the Australian scene. Black and white television became available in the eastern States, in 1956. In 1959, Perth gained its initial single Channel 7, but West Australian country areas like Collie did not start receiving transmissions until 1968.

Those able to buy a set still received an extremely limited program, and spent a lot of time simply watching the test pattern, a marvel in itself. The eastern States could not transmit to Perth directly until 1970, but when the first Apollo 11 moon landing occurred in 1969, a special, complicated series of transmissions were facilitated by the ABC via satellite stations in the U.S. and remote Australia, so excited and amazed West Australians could watch it live through grey, scratchy, blurred screens. Many people around the country could only watch a television placed in a prominent shop-front window in a main street, as Geoff remembers doing. Finally, like many families in Australia in the late 60s, the Fishers became proud owners of a black and white set, a substantial piece of lounge room furniture, but Geoff was away, spreading his wings by that time.

Before television, public entertainments and club activities were frequent and popular, while family members at home played musical instruments, sang, read books, played games, listened to the radio or played records on a gramophone, although some of these activities were not available to families struggling financially. However, for some like Geoff, there were also other kinds of entertainments to be enjoyed.

"In my school years, I preferred all sport. Relationships were too hard. I couldn't get excited about them. There were a few girls who wanted to be my girlfriend, like Jill Henderson and the daughter of Mr. Knight, the pharmacist, but I just saw them as friends. And you had to talk girl-talk! Anyway, I didn't have the confidence to just go for anybody in particular, or to say how I really felt."

High school swimming

Whether in a river or a pool, overall, Geoff used to be the fastest swimmer at school.

"I held one of the school's freestyle records for twenty-five years, until the son of a mining executive, who trained with a squad in Perth, broke my long-standing record. When Collie eventually built a public pool, training really improved for students. But it wasn't heated, so before and after high summer, it was freezing. During high school years, I swam in State Country Championships in Narrogin. I remember winning first place and getting a gold medal for a 100 metres freestyle event, although in the heat, I was one of the slowest swimmers. In the final, I won from lane 8. That was very enjoyable, and the swimming club seemed to hold me in high esteem at the time. They were like a family with lots of kids and their parents, but my parents weren't involved. We trained all the time and had club meets on Sundays.

"Along with other Collie students, I participated in swimming competitions at the 'Crawley Baths' in Perth's Swan River, too. The Crawley Baths were famous for the abundance of sizable jellyfish, with waves coming through the vertical timber boards bobbing around in the water.

"Swimming was always a source of pride and self-confidence – which I was lacking – because I thought I was never good enough for anything else, in particular. In my mind, I wasn't a scholar. I lacked confidence, so I would recklessly challenge things as a way of compensating, as a way of getting past being shy. But I always had a sense of humour throughout my whole school life. If I didn't make the whole class laugh, every day, then it wasn't a good day. Most times I baited the teachers a bit and made them and the whole class laugh. It was like my mission in life, because any time the possibility of a joke came up, I had to express it."

Chapter Fifteen

High school ups and downs

Of course, everybody knew that Geoff was in the Collie Brass Band: "One Anzac Day, the school asked me to play *The Last Post* and *Reveille* on my cornet. I was shaking like a leaf playing solo for the whole school. I liked doing it, but it was a bit traumatic. It provoked anxiety, of course, but I coped alright. I had to play it at one end of the building where the hallways met so the sound could echo through all the spaces. There were a few shaky notes when bashing out *The Last Post*, but I was proud to do that."

When Geoff was in his mid-teens, Jessie bought him a gold trumpet as a gift. "Even second-hand, it would have cost her a lot of dancing lessons to pay for it. (Sixty years later I still have this trumpet.) Later when I was leaving school, I asked my neighbour, George Bury, for a personal reference. He was a service station owner who lived behind us. He commented that on hearing me practising the trumpet over the years, that there were 'always lovely trumpet sounds' coming over – which would have been pretty basic, and I know they really weren't all lovely. They must have been grateful I wasn't playing the drums!"

However, Geoff's music appreciation class at school, held in a pre-fab building, was less active – more theoretical – which did not hold his attention for long.

"We'd listen to a few symphonies, various types of music by well-known composers – that was lovely, but I wasn't that interested in the popular music, like The Beatles. I remember one hot day when I was out of sight behind the piano and the teacher was commanding the class from a raised platform at the front. I took the opportunity to jump out an open window, the large kind of hopper window that opened out at the bottom. I immediately jumped back in and resumed my seat. The trouble was that the other students all looked towards me, so it gave the game away. This resulted in another trip to the headmaster's office.

"Another notable event was when the whole school was lined up at the front of the school. The headmaster's many chins were all shaking as he demanded to know '…who the guttersnipe was who painted on our lovely, powder-blue wall!'. On that wing of the school the culprit had painted in huge letters, 'THE BLOB STRIKES AGAIN!' Someone was supposed to step forward and own up, but there was no movement in the ranks. 'It only takes one rotten apple to spoil the whole basketful!' he said angrily, 'And that guttersnipe – I hope he feels satisfied with himself … blah, blah, blah …' So we all had to endure that. The graffiti referenced a movie on at the Bow Cinema at the time called *The Blob*."

Like most male youth in high schools, Geoff did 'cadets', a military-style training done in army-style uniform on school ovals or yards to teach them a form of structured hierarchical discipline and order. The sub-text to 'cadets training' is that it aims to create a positive readiness for the Australian armed forces, should the need or desire arise. Cadet training involved regular, perfectly synchronised marching. Geoff shares: "I enjoyed breaking the monotony by encouraging the others to go out of step with me, out of time, by dropping one leg lower than the other, so we could have some laughs. Dennis Barron was in charge of us, and he blew a gasket every time!"

Alan, high school cadet, age 15, 1955

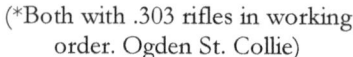

Geoff, high school cadet, 1962

(*Both with .303 rifles in working order. Ogden St. Collie)

Tight finances

In contrast, school excursions promised excitement for Geoff, "…but they involved extra payments that my parents often could not afford. Henry earned about £27 a week, often working two shifts back-to-back in the mine. Henry's double shifts were 7.00am – 3.00pm and 3.00pm – 11.00pm. And sometimes he worked at the weekend."

Until 1966, Australia had British pounds, shillings and pence (pennies) but currency conversion to dollars and cents meant Henry then received about $54 weekly.

Henry's efforts to save those pennies for house costs sometimes clashed with Geoff's mentality, activities, and natural distractions. "I was always told to turn the lights off, and he once wanted to punch my lights out for leaving the radio on all night. I felt a sense of shame that I might hit him, but I restrained myself, and my mother intervened too."

Regardless, a lack of money did not deter Geoff from his personal goals. "I couldn't go on some school excursions, but when the hockey team or football team travelled to Perth for competitions by bus, I'd hitch-hike. Then I'd find them at The Cloisters, and I remember sleeping on the floor in the very front room of the hotel. My friends who had enough money for the accommodation, with a bed, would always let me sleep on the floor. And I'd find the venue where the team was playing and watch a game, then I'd hitch-hike home again.

"We couldn't afford a lot of things. I remember when the Beatles came to Australia, Keith Dewar, my best friend in high school, got a Beatles jacket, and I remember thinking my parents could never afford one, they couldn't just splash out to buy something like that for me – but his mother would probably go without, to make it happen. It was a particular type of jacket made out of artificial fibres – it was terrible, but fashionable, just at that moment in time ... I wouldn't even want one. I didn't get very excited about the Beatles either, but Keith looked interesting, and he was happy.

"One day, Keith, David Palmer and I broke into an old colliery building. They wanted to 'crack' an old safe in the office, but I thought it was a waste of time and wasn't a good idea, so we left it alone. And when I was about sixteen or seventeen, I bought an unregistered second-hand motor scooter. It had no brakes, no lights, a faulty clutch and no muffler, but I enjoyed tearing around the place on it. Joe Turley got angry with me because he said it interfered with his TV reception. I eventually sold it, but not before breaking it down to a thousand pieces and rebuilding it."

When not at school, Geoff was usually busy swimming, playing hockey or tennis, or bike riding with friends.

Geoff in Collie Public Swimming Pool

Geoff (second from right) with Collie swimming team showing medals

Geoff's sports trophies: swimming & cycling

For Geoff, physical activity was completely absorbing and provided a sense of freedom, while building confidence and friendship. However, sometimes there were consequences.

"On one occasion I was driven to recite the Lord's Prayer – even though I didn't really believe it, but I was covering my bets – thought I'd just give it a go. I knew I was going to be in big trouble because I hadn't replenished the wood and coal for the old Metters stove. When I forgot to do things like that, I'd get yelled at, and it came to a head when my father said, 'If you don't start getting everything in on time, I'll do it all myself and you won't get any pocket money!' So, I said 'Okay', then I went off and got a job. From then on, I paid my own school fees and bought everything I needed for high school.

"Trapping rabbits helped. I got a job at Foy's department store bottling kerosene, methylated spirits, and bagging potatoes. I also occasionally helped out on the sweets counter while the girls went to lunch. I helped myself to a considerable amount of chocolate sweets, and Foy's store profits dropped dramatically!"

Robyn was extremely envious of her brother's sweetest of jobs … Soon Geoff obtained his driver's licence, so was able to drive the Foy's delivery van. As he went home at lunchtime to listen to *Blue Hills* on the radio and to have a sandwich with his mother, on one occasion he was able to take home two large discarded cases of condensed milk that were out of date and had become too sugary. He happily recalls drinking them for months.

"Sometimes the store also threw out old sign-boxes with lights and flashing signs, and driving the store van allowed me to give them a new home. I couldn't throw them out because they were just too interesting, and deserved investigating and playing with.

"I also took on a night-shift job during the school holidays at Lyle's timber mill, cutting up lengths of 4-by-2-inch timber on the 'docker'. It didn't last long because I simply couldn't stay awake."

At another time, Geoff worked at a service station serving petrol, topping up oil and checking radiator water levels in people's cars. This kind of service was normal everywhere in the 1950s, 60s and 70s and provided a lot of casual employment for young men like Geoff. Somehow, he managed to juggle school, paid jobs, house chores, adventures, some girls, and a lot of sport.

"I think I gave up the band when I was about sixteen because I was playing too much sport, and I was trying to focus on school. Then Mum gave me a gold trumpet that I still have. The best things about high school were the girls, young teachers, and sport."

In spite of the pleasures and pressures at school, Geoff knew that getting a full high school education was the only reliable way to escape Collie. And, even though there were many things he appreciated in the natural environment there, together with some good neighbours and townspeople, as well as his family, he felt desperate to get out to explore a more challenging world with greater opportunity.

However, his driver's licence provided opportunities for creating a sense of 'total freedom', enhanced by a treasured new motorbike.

Geoff riding his beloved Triumph 650cc Thunderbird 1967

'Born To Be Wild!' Collie 1967

Chapter Sixteen

More about Henry

Geoff agrees with Robyn's description of Henry when she says, "Henry was about 5' 10" (178 cms). Near the end of high school, Geoff was taller than him at 6' (183 cm). Henry had a very solid physique, but he wasn't fat at all. He was very proud, standing very upright. He spoke very well, with a slight English accent, but he could also swear like a trooper! Although he liked music and said he could play the violin, our family didn't see any evidence of this. He really didn't have a good ear for music, but he loved Kamahl, who he said had 'a voice as rich as fruit cake.'

Geoff adds, "I admired my father's tenacity and the fact that he would put his family first. And he was street wise. He told us that, as a kid in England, he sold newspapers, old editions, to make a few pence. He said people would realize he'd sold them yesterday's edition after they'd gone down the street!" Geoff describes more of Henry's adult skills that he admired, saying "… how he could stop an electricity meter with a magnet, and how he created lighting in the front yard in Boulder by soldering a couple of wires to a huge light bulb of about 500 watts, probably from the mine, and just dropping it onto the power lines out the front before the meter. That made a great outside light. He was up to lots of tricks, here and there.

"He knew a lot. His special skills inspired me to try a few things, too. I learnt how to tap our home phone with a set of old Bakelite headphones left over from World War II. I could listen to calls coming into the house, and could pretend I was an ASIO operative … maybe I imagined I was part of my favourite radio detective serial, *Night Beat*. Then people got suspicious when they heard crackling sounds on the line, so I had to desist.

"Henry made his own Besser bricks to build the back verandah. And inside the backyard garage, he built a pit for fixing his cars. It had a little ladder and a little loft above."

Robyn recalls, "One day, our Scolari neighbours lost a piglet – it had gone missing. I think someone accused Henry of taking it, which he wouldn't have admitted. I believe the piglet had escaped and gone into the back lane, where Henry found it, and could have simply thought 'finders, keepers!' In fact, he had then put it in the car pit where he kept it and fattened it up for a few weeks. It was then cooked with delicious crackling, plenty of fat, and eaten over several meals, but I refused to eat it, knowing where it came from."

Geoff particularly admired Henry's practical skills and versatility. "He built a trailer from scratch with the help of a friend who was a welder. He was very capable. And then he got into bee-hives and was making money with them, part-time. He liked duck-shooting. That was his sport, and it provided food for the family too. And he also used to go to the gun club in Collie, in his 50s and 60s, shooting clay pidgeons. He had a flat-bottomed canoe he had made for duck shooting which impressed my friends. It would float in a couple of inches of water because of its flat bottom, but it was a bit unstable and dangerous for normal canoeing. I used to take it down to the river a lot. I was interested in a lot of things he did, like how he fixed things.

"And I was impressed by my father's gardening, how he could do things, like change a variety of plum tree from one to another by grafting. My father was always gardening. That was his thing. He had a whole backyard full of fresh produce. I helped him a little bit in the garden. It's funny how genetics must have some bearing on things, because I used to see acorns in the back lane. We used to play in the back lane all the time as little kids. I always wondered about them growing, and I was fascinated by them, and it made me think of them growing in England somewhere.

"My world view was shaped by nature and what I saw in my childhood. I used to admire the moon a lot, and the fog, and the cold still nights, and the ice on the ducks' and chooks' water and taps breaking because they were full of ice, and the hose snapping off.

"In the early 60s, Henry was a member of the miners' union and became their secretary for a while. However, he warned me against 'this politician, this guy in the Trade Unions, who is a bit left-wing and could have leanings toward Communism'. His name was Bob Hawke! And he warned me against being seen with our swimming coach, Bill Latter, saying I would never get a government job if I was seen with this so-called Communist. I listened to that advice, then ignored it. I was just taught to be scared of Communism, as was everyone else in the western world at that time, thinking we might have to get under our desks at school one day, 'when the bomb goes off!' It wasn't all that long after World War II when Japan got bombed. The Cold War between U.S.A. and the Soviet Union threatened nuclear attacks, so anything was a possibility.

"Henry joined the Freemasons at the local Lodge, with all

the secret handshakes and special gear they wore. He didn't tell us much about it, but he went there quite a lot."

Henry in Freemason outfit.

"The first car in my memory that he had was a Ford Prefect, which was such a little car. We'd sit in the back to go to Perth from Collie, and it seemed to take at least five hours. He would pull the engine out, repair and service it, and I would be watching everything.

"When I was seven or eight, he stored a 44-gallon drum of petrol in the garage and that was fine until Janis and I got caught lighting fires near it, as we experimented with matches. He was so angry that he nearly hit me with a grape vine cutting, so Janis and I had to run like mad past him to get back to the safety of the house!"

Family stories about Henry convey his characteristic, ready sense of humour. He liked to exaggerate the truth, perform practical jokes, and tell amusing, tall tales. He was often quite naughty, given the opportunity!

Robyn relates an anecdote of Henry's about when he was a cook in an army camp during World War II, based in Cowra, NSW. "His story was that one night, everyone complained about the food, so the next night he went out and collected a cow pat and put it in the big pot of beef stew, and they all loved it! Another story about his army experience was that he and his mates, more than once, would go out to another camp to steal tyres with a big, long pole. Then they would thread the tyres on the pole and carry it on their shoulders back to their own camp. What they did with the tyres is somewhat of a mystery, but we gather they sold them on the black market. The military police were a bit confused when searching for the culprit, mistakenly looking for a 'Sergeant Cook' instead of Sergeant Fisher."

Henry Fisher (centre)

Henry Fisher with beret, Cowra N.S.W (c. 1941ss-1942)

Geoff also remembers, "Henry told me that, one weekend, when he went camping with his mates, and while they were sleeping, he partly buried a full-sized latex hand in the sand. He placed it at the water's edge, in front of their tents with most of it jutting up from the surface. When they clambered out in the morning and saw it, bleary-eyed, they went from shock to belly laughter as they realized it was just another one of Henry's practical jokes." Geoff had given his father the hand as a gift.

In contrast, Robyn remembers adventures as a young teenager when "… Henry would take me out in his 'tinny' with oars to illegally drop marron traps in the river, and pull them up after dark. He taught me how to row the boat silently, not even dripping any water from the oars, very, very slowly. The marron were huge back then and very tasty. They were cooked, and some were pickled." (No doubt, even tastier as ill-gotten gains!)

Geoff recalls Henry's building activities. "In the late 1950s,

Henry decided to modernise the house, so with my help, we took off all the weatherboards and replaced them with fashionable, smooth, new, beautiful asbestos sheets. We had to carry them and cut them to fit. In those days, protection from asbestos fibres was unheard of. We also painted our very steep roof, somewhat daunting due to the long drop to earth. Alan may have helped too."

In addition, Henry had built a brick garage at the side of the house with Geoff's help.

24 Ogden Road, Collie

Concerning tensions in the home, Geoff shares, "Some conflicts with my father made me angry, but I never felt hate towards him. I only hated that he argued with my mother, because it went on and on through our whole childhood, everyday at 6.30 a.m. when the fire had been stoked and re-lit, and breakfast made. They would argue about how hot the breakfast was – eggs too cold, or the cup of tea too cold – so breakfast time was a 'battle-station'. But they would argue any time. And he would just yell ... As kids, we were trying to hide, to close our ears. Even with our fingers in our ears, with all the yelling and carrying on we could still hear them going at it from the next room.

"My mother must have been very depressed at times. She never got over Alan's suicide. She used to get migraines, as Robyn also does. My father was in pain with gout, and sore from working in all the jobs he did."

Henry suffered gout from about fifty years of age. Robyn adds, "Because of this, in the middle of winter, he put the heater on so very hot, while our mother was going through her 'change of life' – plus he was going deaf, so he'd have the TV turned up loud and it was actually quite unbearable! She suffered a lot, but then he suffered too. We can't just say everything was his fault."

Robyn's experience of their arguments matches Geoff's, and no doubt Janis's, but Robyn also remembers that sometimes, when the arguments were usually going on very early in the morning or at night, "... that either Geoff or Janis, or both of them together, would put a pillow over my head so that I couldn't hear. So, I've spent years having suffocation dreams. Sometimes I would, for no apparent reason, feel that I couldn't breathe."

In Robyn's opinion, "Henry and Jessie would have a good time when other people were around, having a few drinks, but underneath all that, they were two sad people. She blamed him for Alan's death. She always blamed him. I remember one day when we were both hanging out the washing together. It was Alan's anniversary, and she said, 'It was all your father's fault!' I reacted with, 'Don't tell me that, I don't want to hear it!' I think I was trying to protect Henry."

Geoff, 9 years old with Jessie, Henry, Janis and baby Robyn, Ogden Street, Collie

Henry smoked most of his life, together with Jessie, many of their relatives and friends, and almost everyone around them, although none of the Fisher offspring did. As smoking used to be a common lifestyle activity in Australia and around the world, people were free – even encouraged – to smoke in shared spaces such as in cinemas, theatres, restaurants, buses, trains, and planes. Everywhere, ashtrays were built into our public venues for common use … so hard to imagine now!

Regarding Henry's work, which would have challenged his health, Geoff says, "Henry worked at various mines in Collie, the last being the Collie Co-Op Mine on the edge of town, not far from the Collie Hotel. We can still go down the mine to about 300 metres, as a tour. In 1960, Collie's mines were taken over by Amalgamated Collieries. In 1970, one day before his sixty-first birthday, he retired with a pension."

Geoff went to Collie when Henry died of liver cancer in Collie on 9th April 1977, aged sixty-six. "I remember visiting him in hospital to see him one last time. He looked very serene. I kissed him on his forehead and tried to make sense of his passing."

Chapter Seventeen

More about Jessie

"Jessie was about 5'7" and slim with a good figure before her middle-age years. She was very active, always dancing, riding her bike to do shopping or doing housework. I used to try to please my mother. I'd polish the floor with Fisher's Wax on the three-brush polisher. I'd have it ready and shining before Millie King came to visit, a bespectacled woman from the other side of town who was married to the owner of the hardware store. Mr King used to play ragtime music on his old piano at home when we visited them, many times."

Robyn is in Jessie's image, as photos attest, and she often talks, jokes and laughs just like her.

Geoff always enjoyed Jessie's jokes and expressions. "I was encouraged by my mother's sense of humour. She had a wicked sense of humour and she was naughty!"

"Her sister, my Aunty Dot, had a good sense of humour too. When Aunty Dot came to visit, they would sit up all night drinking sweet sherry and smoking cigarettes and they'd gas-bag about everything and nothing, or whatever I wasn't privy to, because they'd make sure all the kids were out of earshot.

Mardon sisters - Beryl, Dorothy (Dot), Jessie

Robyn muses, "Jessie was very funny and laughed a lot, often making jokes about people. She loved to say 'bastard' in a joking way, in phrases like, 'Thank Christ that bastard's gone!', when some possibly difficult or possibly pleasant male person left the house." And like Geoff, Robyn also remembers the many times Jessie sat out on the front verandah with Aunty Dot or a friend, chatting endlessly and laughing, often saying, 'Thank God – now I've got a bit of time to myself!'

According to Geoff, "She also frequently said, 'I'll have to make a long belt for Henry to attach the many things that he loses all the time!' And Jessie loved to get Henry out of the house so that she could clean it to her heart's content."

Apparently the 'lino' (linoleum) floor was always so perfectly clean, one could – proverbially - 'eat off it', and the same applied to the floor boards. The old, basic Simpson washing machine with its wringer that Geoff remembers was inclined to produce frequent little electric shocks with all the water around, was always working, constantly washing Henry's coal-blackened work clothes. This could only happen after Jessie had first rubbed them vigorously on her washboard. Jessie was also always darning socks, mending generally, or sewing clothes and household items on her vintage treadle Singer sewing machine.

Robyn adds, "When not too busy, in a moment of rest, she enjoyed stepping outside to look at her favourite hydrangeas and geraniums, and she really loved to watch the funny behaviour of the chooks."

Reflecting further on Jessie, Geoff says, "The only time I got upset with my mother, in my early teens, was when she tried to make me wear a cardigan when I was going off to the movies. I just didn't want to be seen in a cardigan! We'd wrangle over it and we could be seen yelling at each other in the middle of the street, until Mum thought she had won the battle, but I'd drop it off at David Palmer's house and pick it up later. I was prepared to make my own way and suffer my own consequences. And she was always putting extra army blankets (left-overs from World War II) on my bed on a cold night, whether I wanted them or not. I didn't need the blankets, but I guess it was her way of caring for me."

"My mother was a very good dancer. She had won trophies and prizes in ballroom dancing competitions in Kalgoorlie before we moved to Collie. Then she taught everyone who got married in the Collie area. She taught them to do the bridal waltz and other ballroom dances. She always kept that going, and it was another source of income for her. Originally, everyone had to pay something like 2/6d for an hour's lesson, Monday to Friday nights from 6.00 to 7.00 p.m. And sometimes she taught down in one of the halls. She would scatter the sawdust with a sprinkling of kerosene on the jarrah-wooden floor to make it slide-able. I went to dancing lessons for a little bit too, but I really just didn't want to do it. I wasn't very excited about it. She was very disappointed that I didn't want to progress to competitions for medals and prizes."

Robyn recalls that Jessie also taught dancing to girls at the local Catholic school, and occasionally the girls were allowed to dance with local Catholic school boys for partnered lessons - so they knew what the real thing was like!

Geoff continues, "She competed regularly in the South-West Ballroom Championships and regularly competed in Bunbury. She had a lot of medals and everyone knew about her. She won gold, silver and bronze medals, always competing with dance partner, Clive Dornay."

Jessie and dance partner, Clive Dornay, in competition

"My father wasn't excited about dancing as recreation, but sometimes they'd dance at the Collie Workers' Club – they'd jump around, get pissed, and then come home and argue."

Henry and Jessie, Collie Workers Club

In later years - Henry and Jessie, Collie Workers' Club

"And for many years, Henry went duck shooting and camping with his mates some weekends on Saturdays while Jessie went dancing or stayed home with the children.

"At home, I used to listen to Mum's music. She collected music for every dance, like the Gay Gordon, Pride of Erin, Canadian Two Step, Polkas, the Waltz, Barn Dance, Fox Trot and Quick Step, mostly on small vinyl 45's. There were classical pieces too, as well as popular tunes by Bing Crosby, Dean Martin, and others. She also played it for us when we were sick. She had lots of music that I enjoyed. But when it was going on and on all the time with the dancing lessons, I had to get out of the place."

Robyn's experience of the situation was rather different: "I thought it was great because I had the house to myself, when I could climb up the cupboard and get the cough mixture and have a sip!"

Robyn used to do her homework in the evenings while Jessie's music was playing so, like Geoff and Janis, felt forever connected to it. However, she remembers that sometimes their exhausted mother came inside at the end of a dancing session saying, 'God, that bastard had two left feet!' - by which the family understood it was impossible to teach some people to dance, even with her most expert tuition.

Jessie had a moneybox to put her dancing lesson earnings in, being only 2/6d per person. In 1966, she had to convert the fee to about $4.50 as Australia adopted its new decimal currency. Robyn remembers that the money earned paid for Jessie's dresses, adding, "She liked to go to 'the dress shop' owned by Mrs Swindell and once she bought the most beautiful, exquisite long dress, then bought the same one in all the different colours, so that nobody else could wear one to the same event as her."

Geoff's vision of Jessie, when prepared for dancing or for special events of any kind, was that, "She plastered on make-up with a mountain of lipstick, often bright red, and teased up her variously dyed hair with loads of Gossamer hairspray that smelled awful, and had such an artificial look." Throughout his life, Geoff has not understood the need for women to use such heavy makeup.

However, Robyn was more impressed than Geoff by Jessie's individual presentation and dress style, saying, "She used to dye her own hair. She would go from a red to a brown, darker and lighter. One day Henry came home from work and said that one of the guys at lunchtime in the mine had said, 'What colour is your wife's hair today, Henry?' and he said, 'I don't know, I haven't seen her since 7.00 a.m.!' And she was the only person I know who could do a perfect high French Roll."

Robyn continues to relate another of Jessie's amusing behaviours. "And she liked to have a little sip of sherry. An old, local Italian guy used to make his own and he would come around in his truck every Thursday. She would go down the front steps with her big plastic basket, tall with rounded handles, that two flagons fitted in perfectly. She would hand over the empty ones, and he would put the full ones in the big basket and she would pay him. She always thought that when she was doing that, she could see the curtains moving in the neighbours' windows, and that they'd be saying: 'Ah, Jessie's buying her sherry again!' She loved the taste of sherry, but later in life she mixed water with it, and didn't drink to get drunk at home."

Geoff fondly remembers his mother going out and about on her bike, adding, "Jessie didn't have a driving licence, so rode her bike to do errands or to visit people. I remember watching her riding her bike with the little dynamo on the front wheel, a small headlight and a tail light, for night riding. When shopping, she always rode off with her string bag hanging off the handlebars, but if she had to buy a heavy load, she would walk the bike home. She eventually got her driver's licence in her forties, so she could exercise a little more independence - in her little Austin 1100."

Jessie was then able to visit her mother Daisy in Victoria Park more easily.

Geoff's grandmother, Daisy Mardon – at home in Victoria Park

According to Robyn, "A couple of years after Henry's death, Jessie went to hospital to have an artificial pig's valve put into her heart. She had aortic stenosis. Her doctor told her to stop smoking, relax and look after herself. Just before this she was making her own floor polish in the kitchen, I think from beeswax, and she had some melting on the stove. It suddenly boiled over and burnt all of her arm, so she ran next door to the neighbours and they took her to hospital to get her arm dressed. Apparently, the fright of all this set her heart off, leading to the bypass, although her death certificate shows 'generalised arteriosclerosis'. As long as I can remember, she polished her own floor, and also the dance hall floor where she taught dancing."

"After her heart operation, she appeared well and continued to teach dancing at home, also going out every Saturday night to dance, maintaining her usual lifestyle. However, about one year later, she decided to go to her much-loved Collie Workers' Club. On Saturday nights they always had a three-piece band and everyone danced and drank and smoked. So, Jessie had a shandy and a fag - because she just couldn't do what she was told! Her heart gave up the next day. I think Jessie possibly had a heart murmur all her life, but she had developed a clot and had a heart arrest when she was alone at home. Jessie died on 6th July 1980 at 61 years of age, just one week before her 62nd birthday."

Geoff adds, "Jess was a good mother, caring and proud of us kids. She loved motherhood, but I'm sure it wore her down, along with the duties of being a dutiful wife."

"Both Henry and Jessie were life-long smokers. Jessie's sister, our Aunty Dot, with our Uncle Harry, always smoked too, and he had a hacking cough that would go on so long, it sounded as if he couldn't get a breath and would die any minute."

Chapter Eighteen

A bit about siblings

Relationships

About his brother Alan, Geoff says, "I admired that my brother had horses and motorbikes … and then I was traumatised by his suicide. It was very painful for me. I became the 'big brother' to the two girls and I was always aware of that, especially as I got older. I didn't feel like a middle child any more, but my parents didn't talk to me about that sort of thing – or the traumatic death."

Although Robyn adores and trusts both Geoff and Janis, Geoff's relationship with Janis seems to have been subject to some sibling rivalry, more common when siblings are close in age. For example, Robyn recalls that Jessie often let the children help make bread dough, which they enjoyed doing, but once annoyed, Geoff was known to call the product of Janis's effort 'polio pastry'.

Reflecting the impact of the polio pandemic in early 1950s Australia, children often used related terms negatively, like 'spastic', to taunt each other.

Geoff recalls, "We often quarrelled when it was time to wash and dry the dishes. One time when I was calling Janis names and we were annoying each other, Janis hit me just above the eye with a saucepan, leaving a scar that took about thirty years to disappear."

In contrast, the positive rapport between Geoff and Robyn was mutual, and it may have been an easy relationship because they were nine years apart, having a fond 'big brother' and 'little sister' relationship. As Geoff says, "Robyn was always an entertaining and cute little kid."

Robyn comments further with, "I always felt very safe with Geoff. I had a lot of confidence in his abilities and his care for me. He was never awful to me, he never made me feel unwanted. I adored Geoff. He was a good looking, nice person. He never swore. He used to ride around the velodrome a lot. Early on, we didn't have a television, and later we didn't watch it that much, although I remember we watched my first movie on it, *Dr Jekyll and Mr Hyde*, and I thought it was really creepy ... I still do. We didn't just lay around while our parents were working or dancing. We were always doing something, and often together."

Humour

Robyn recalls, "Every New Year's Eve, our parents went out to Don Pike's house, who owned the abattoir, and rode an old horse called Butch. So, every New Year's Eve, Geoff and Janis had to look after me. One of these times, Roddy Dransfield, a neighbour and female friend of Geoff's, and Keith Dewar were also with us. I think I was six at the time. They all took me down the street and around the corner to the big red public telephone box. They made me phone up 'the speaking clock', letting me think there was a real person on the other end, so I tried talking to them and couldn't. Then they laughed at me and I realized they were tricking me, but I thought it was funny too."

The 'Speaking Clock' was a free public phone service (on

a wired, landline phone) with voice recordings of the exact time, saying for example, 'At the third stroke, it will be ten twenty five and fifty seconds.' It never stopped or altered the message format. It was valued when people did not have their own watches, when mobiles and computers did not exist.

Robyn continues, "Then they played tricks on the old couple's house, a few doors down the road. After tying black cotton to the creaky wire door, they ran and hid across road, and pulled on the wire door to open it, then released it to slam shut. When the old couple came out to check, they couldn't see anything and went back inside, confused, only for Geoff and his friends to do it again. Really pleased with their success, they'd go off laughing madly until the practical joke lost its impact and we all went on to the next thing."

Geoff comments, "We all have a similar sense of humour - often black humour. I remember, even when our father was dying, Janis and I cracked up over a joke we made, which must have been about dying, because we were hysterical with laughter. It was probably also a good release. Generally speaking, we're all different, maybe because we all had different fathers – we know that because our parents used to make humorous references to the baker!"

Music

While Geoff enjoyed learning to play his own choice of musical instruments, his sisters both learned to play the piano. "Robyn had lessons with the nuns who made it difficult for her to continue lessons with confidence, by rapping her over the knuckles with a ruler when she made mistakes." Nevertheless, she also greatly enjoys music. And Robyn adds, "Janis continued to learn music and to play piano very well and, like Geoff, has always loved opera."

Music is a joyful, intrinsic part of all their lives.

Sweets

While all living in Collie, the Fishers were fixated on sweets of all kinds. They had dessert every night. Jessie regularly made jelly and ice-cream, wine trifles, fruit, pumpkin or sponge cakes with lashings of cream. Much of this tradition has been handed down from Jessie's mother, Daisy, and on to Robyn.

Just saying the word 'cream' gets Geoff and Robyn excited. Once triggered, one or two spoonsful are never enough! If ice-cream or custard is left over, they will usually find a way to finish it off. Of course, wine trifle is most exciting because it has almost everything in one dish.

As Robyn admits, "We don't know when we're full. We have to feel sick to stop. We definitely have an obsession with cream, honey, carnation milk, chocolate, cake, ice-cream, and any lollies, especially liquorice. Janis no longer eats all that stuff to excess, choosing to eat and live as healthily as possible, except when she gets her hands on Cherry Ripes or Liquorice Allsorts – she's got it too, but not as bad!"

On a healthier front, all siblings tried out a range of different sports. The high school used the town's 50-metre pool and 'Mrs Murray' had previously trained Geoff for swimming competitions there. Robyn tried netball for a while, but didn't really like it, so hoped to achieve better with her swimming skills, but when she swam the whole pool length, felt like she was drowning. As she reached the end of the pool, breathless, gasping, she heard Mrs Murray say: 'Well, you'd never believe she was Geoff's sister!' Robyn believes

Geoff and Janis are more physically adept at sport, although they all have very active lifestyles.

Previous and present Fishers have always felt connected to natural environments, whether land or sky, ocean or river, flora or fauna - wild or domestic. Whenever possible, they have followed their desire to travel to locations near and far, often to enjoy dramatic and beautiful landscapes. Even at home, still her father's daughter, Robyn created a wild, lush jungle of banana trees and other plants, surrounding a productive vegetable patch, all beside chook and duck pens, watched over by her dogs and other incidental pets. [While completing this biography, Robyn has decided to downsize and has had to let go of her jungle and wildlife, handing it all over to others excited to inherit it. Now she is busy planting in every little nook and cranny at her new home.]

Although Geoff rarely engages in gardening himself, he enjoys the beauty of the colour and creative arrangement of plants, together with the edible bounty of his home gardens, always supporting Toni in her horticultural pursuits.

When travelling in Australia, Geoff has sensitively photographed visually rich regions and its characters. Equally unique images have been captured of curious or heart-warming scenes of people in foreign lands - in their amazing ancient or modern settings. Our seemingly infinite Indian Ocean has always been a favourite source for appealing images, many with friends exercising and socialising, or in swimming events, and frequently for spirited family portraits. A great many are also of his family 'beaching' on the West Australian coastline locally, or holidaying beyond.

In this context, it is worth noting that Janis has lived in Hawaii since 1975 on the island of Kauai in a lush, rugged landscape by the ocean, working in wildlife conservation with her husband, and taking nature tours – while living as sustainably as possible.

The sporty, mature siblings: (L to R) Janis, Geoff and Robyn

Chapter Nineteen

Moving on

"Near the end of high school, my father, in his forties, came to my vocational counselling session in a blue suit with flared trousers and his thinning hair neatly combed. The counsellor recommended a trade, which was pretty spot-on. But then a brochure turned up about cadetships for reporters for The West Australian newspaper, and on the back, there was a mention of cadetships in photography."

"I thought that sounded just like me. However, I was doing my best to keep my options open, so I applied for different jobs and training programs that I thought were possibilities, including for a CBA bank clerk position with Mr Nuttall, the bank manager, and for primary school teacher training. In those days, everything was a possibility. I ignored all positive replies, except for the cadet photographer position in Perth. In January 1967, I rang up the West Australian and got through to the photography department and spoke to the boss, an ex-World War II Airforce pilot, Douglas J. Burton. He said, 'When you're in Perth next, drop in to see us and have a chat.'"

"So a week later, I got my father to drop me off on the outskirts of Collie and hitch-hiked to Perth, found my way to the photography department, only to discover that Douglas J. Burton was in Melbourne ... so I hitch-hiked back to Collie again. I made an appointment for a week later by phone, and once again hitch-hiked to Perth where my in-person application was successful!"

"When I graduated from high school, I was breaking my neck to get out of town. I was going to 'high-tail it' at my first opportunity, so as soon as a job came through, I was off to Perth. My parents used to argue all the time, so I was glad to escape.

"Then, for my cadetship employment in Perth, I got a room near Beatty Park, in Newcastle Street. The landlady was a Mrs Mack, with thick glasses and an always startled appearance. She spent her days following horse races on radio, 'ghost betting'. She'd put on bets without actually spending any money, just pretending – like some people do 'ghost betting' on the share market, to see how good they are."

Geoff, Cadet Press photographer at The West Australian 1967... "Just loved my skinny black ties and Glo-Weave short sleeved shirts in those days ... not to mention shorts and long socks. Fortunately, I haven't discovered photos with my 'safari suit'."

"Anyway, I stayed there for about a year, then moved to share a one-bedroom unit next to the ABC in Adelaide Terrace in the CBD with Keith Dewar, my high school friend. He was doing school teacher training. Later he moved to another share house in Claremont, and I moved to North Perth. Then 'his number came up' – he was called up for national service – and mine didn't. Sadly, he was blown up in Vietnam, and came back in a box to be buried in Collie. We had shared many of our teenage years, just hanging out, waiting for this time to pass so that we could get to adulthood and the promise of more exciting days. And motorbikes. And much more. What a sad ending for such a beautiful guy."

Water polo

In 1968, when Geoff was living and working in Perth, he decided to try water polo and joined the Dolphins Water Polo Club. "The coach was a plumber, Stan Hammond, who used to scream at us in an immeasurable level of decibels, things like 'You're fucking useless!' I didn't appreciate that aggression, but I enjoyed the sport itself. It was a whole new game. But team sports are really good because you learn teamwork.

"Injuries were occasional, but once I was elbowed in the face by a fellow nicknamed 'Elbows', for obvious reasons, in an A-Reserve Grand Final. He was a former coach of the Dockers Football Club in Perth. Everybody knows who he is – but not because of his sportsmanship. It was difficult to forgive that injury, as it was selfishly and maliciously done, especially as I had lost my mouthguard a week before at Beatty Park. At the point of injury, I didn't know if I had any teeth left in my mouth or not, and for the next week, my mouth was numb. I had to have two root-canals due to deadened nerves in those teeth. It cost me $1,200 which was very expensive at the time. I didn't have much respect for someone who would do that."

In spite of this, Geoff continued to keep water polo in his sporting life with many good team friends.

Learning photography

Geoff was a newspaper cadet for two years, from 1967 to 1969. He was happy with his new lifestyle in Perth. He took up Judo for a while, and played a lot of hockey. He also played ten-pin bowling and went to the pub now and again with friends, as young men did.

Cadet on the job

Perth 1969

"I enjoyed my job and always wanted to make good images. I learned from other experienced photographers. I was taught to develop black and white negatives, which I could do with my eyes closed – it's done in a darkroom anyway. I learnt on an old Speed Graphic press camera with 5x4 inch film, as seen in the old Superman movies. The Speed Graphic is a most amazing camera. There were over thirty photographers at The West Australian in those days, plus two technicians, and a head photographer."

"On assignment we were given Lambretta motor scooters with a box on the back for our cameras. We would ride all over the place. At Fremantle, we'd meet an old guy called Bruce Lee and he would have planned a list of about twenty-five to thirty or more photo shoots to do all over the Fremantle area, all booked for us to go from one to another. We'd always be running late and he'd be out the front, shaking his jowls, because he had quite a big, loose face that flapped when he shook his head ... and we were always in trouble, and always laughing about it. One of us cadets would be down there every Friday, and he'd give us the list and off we'd go. We'd be finding little shops in alleys and boarding ships in the port, meeting people here and there. I'd complete all those jobs and race back to St George's Terrace. We were taught to work quickly so I'd develop the film and carefully print all the pictures and caption them and still leave for home by 5pm."

"We served the Fremantle Gazette, the community newspaper owned by The West Australian. 'WA Newspapers' was an umbrella corporation for a wide range of publications in the State."

The climb

"Each day when I left 'The West' office, I walked out of the photography department through various routes, sometimes past the linotype operators still using a process with hot metals forming the type, down more stairs and sometimes exiting at the publishing bay where the delivery trucks lined up. By this time I was in a laneway leading out to a big car park. Then I'd go looking for my motorbike. One day I left my keys back in the office. Well, the building's walls have these little indentations of about three centimetres – if that. I decided I wasn't going to walk all the way around, up the laneway, up the stairs, along the corridors ... so I just went up the wall about three floors. I got to a narrow window that was hardly big enough to climb through, and I think it was Alan Rowe who was gazing out at the trees at the level of the power lines, when he found my face suddenly at the window. And he couldn't open the window quickly enough. It was a little window with an old-fashioned latch. He grabbed my arm and pulled me in. Other photographers were looking over his shoulder – they were all pretty gob-smacked. I went up there with leather shoes on – not the ideal climbing shoes. It was just one of those things you do in your youth, at nineteen or twenty. That was the talk of the office for the rest of the day!"

"I was able to meet a lot of interesting people as a photographer, people like Liza Minelli, here for a show, and other odd international celebrities and famous Australians. We'd also photograph events, such as the cricket or the Speedway, which was great."

Harmonicas

"I went on a car trip north to Port Hedland with fellow cadet, Joe Willner. I took a harmonica and worked out how to play it on the trip. It was a driving holiday in his Mum's EH Holden. We camped out along the way, driving north as far as Exmouth. I was able to drive Joe crazy, learning to play! Later, I bought a more complicated chromatic mouth organ to play all the half-notes, which was more complex and interesting. I didn't just play chords, I played notes, picking out a song, then putting a little base in with it. I could play the melody and put in a rhythm with the lower notes. Whatever I heard, I could play. With the trumpet, I learnt to play with sheet music. In later years, I took possession of a piano accordion that Ross Louthean's Aunty Jean gave me, and had some fun with that. Ross was a mining journalist I worked and travelled through the Goldfields with in 1970."

Out and about for The West

"The job at The West Australian was very exciting. The first photographer I went on an assignment with was Thomas J. Dann. We went to Dalkeith to photograph Miss Australia, Tania Verstak (now Tania Young). She was gorgeous! In subsequent years, my mother-in-law, Anne, played bridge with her mother. A cadet photographer's job was diverse because it involved the morning West Australian, the afternoon Daily News, the Countryman for regional areas and some work for the Women's Weekly magazine."

Geoff on the job for The West Australian

"I often worked from 7 am to 3 pm, but on the way to work, I went to the post office, the big G.P.O. (General Post Office) in Forrest Place in the Perth CBD. The G.P.O was part of the process because the internet didn't exist and the only way to get pictures was 'over the wire'. Down in the basement of the G.P.O., we collected the 'picture-grams (big negatives) still wet having just arrived 'off the wire'. Then I took them to the darkrooms at the West Australian and printed them on an enlarger. I had to put each wet negative between two pieces of glass, remove all the bubbles and make a print onto photographic paper with the enlarger. Then I had to roll up the prints, and send them up 'the tube' to the picture editor for the Daily News. These photos had to make the first edition of the country edition of the Daily News, so that places like Collie would see them by 3 pm the same day.

Finally, I had to prepare mixed chemicals, then go on further photographic shoots."

"Another time, I went to a party that carried on all night and went straight to work that early morning. So, I was really tired at the end of the work day, but when I was about to go home, the Chief of Staff that day, a guy called Herbie Martin (trained as a 'Dam-Buster in WWII), gave me another assignment to do. Later, on the way back to the office, a signpost jumped out and hit the Cortina I was driving – I was falling asleep. The office suspended my WA newspaper company carpool driving licence for a period of time. That was a difficult day."

The Daily News

"I requested to be a reporter and was transferred to the Daily News staff. When working in the newsroom, shared by the Daily News and The West, I worked from 3 am to about 10 am. One particular night, I photographed models at a modelling academy owned by the ex-wife of a man named Hugh Schmidt who ran the news bureau. I went home, in Nedlands, with one of the models, then drove her home to Belmont, then went home and fell asleep fully dressed, knowing that I would have to get up in a couple of hours for work, with a 'wake-up reminder call' from the PMG phone service.

"At the news bureau, I had to get the first news bulletin out for radio 6PR and other media after which I went downstairs, opened up the darkroom, developed all the photos from the Model Academy session and left them half produced, then went back upstairs to get another bulletin out. I had to go downstairs again to finish off all the prints and close the darkroom down in time for a former cadet colleague to open up at 7 am. With my work in the newsroom completed, I went home at 10 am - pretty tired!"

"When I was working on the Daily News in 1969 or 1970, I met a reporter there, John Murphy, who I would see pacing up and down the hallway between The West and the Daily News, muttering to himself. Earlier in 1969, a photographer colleague, Kevin Davidson, had offered me a 12-gauge sawn-off shotgun that had belonged to John. It had been taken away from him, as it was considered too dangerous for him to have in the 'police rounds' car when the police were looking for a serial murderer named Eric Edgar Cooke."

"So, I became the new owner of this 12-gauge shotgun with a falling block hammer that must be pulled back with a thumb, like out of Davy Crocket, or a western movie. It was legal but very old-fashioned. It could blow a huge hole into something, or someone. John had the gun for self-protection because he was out roaming the streets at night, looking for the serial murderer with the police and others, but he was more likely to kill himself with it!"

Cooke had caused terror in the hearts and minds of people in Perth from 1959 to 1963. When Cooke, a working, married family man with a repaired but disfiguring hair lip and cleft palate, was finally arrested for his crimes, our mother Anne, as one of only a few clinical psychologists in Perth, was employed by the judicial court to assess him at the prison and provide a report.

At this point in Geoff's story, we may ponder the synchronicity of crossed paths, or 'six degrees of separation' when he says, "Little did I know that I was going to meet John again at my future mother-in-law's, and many times thereafter!" (All will be revealed …)

"A couple of years later, working for the Daily News, I had to write stories in time for the first edition by 8.30 am. Later, I'd amble across the Terrace with other reporters to the Palace Hotel for a couple of beers, for morning tea. Then we'd go back to work to finish everything for the day

Taking a work break for another family visit
Grandma Daisy, Geoff, Jessie, Collie

Chapter Twenty

Freelancing

"I went up to the Daily News in 1969, but left in August, 1970. I chose to leave WA Newspapers for a life of freelancing. I thought I was very good at not being a very good reporter! I had enthusiam, but didn't think I managed the required research very well. In those days, you could decide what you wanted to do and just do it, even if you weren't very good at it. It was a great experience, but I decided to take a break and go down south on a canoe trip with my cousin's husband, Kevin Tapper. We did a big five-day canoe trip on the Blackwood River in rain and high water, camping each night amongst the trees and sleeping in hammocks. After that I freelanced work for The Sunday Times and Lang Hancock's Sunday Independent."

Goldfields

Soon Geoff made a plan to go 'over-east' with a mining journalist colleague, Ross Louthean. As it happened, Kalgoorlie was the first stop on the way, so they stayed there and worked, but they also roamed the surrounding goldfields, freelancing for about six months. For their base, they rented a share house in Kalgoorlie, just a couple of streets away from the infamous Hay Street brothels.

House-mate reporters Geoff and Ross Louthean
Kalgoorlie 1970

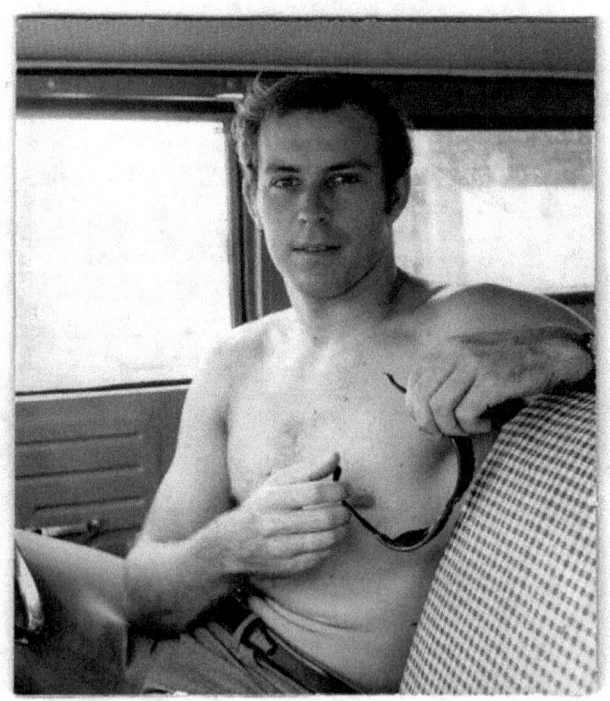

Geoff, freelance reporter, WA Goldfields 1970

"We thought all our Christmases had come at once in the middle of the night when we heard there was a fire in the brothel nearby. We rushed over there, fully expecting to photograph naked women running for their lives, but the fire turned out to be in an old-people's home – behind the brothel. We wrote the fire story and made the Daily News deadline in time, while their staff reporter, Stewart Richmond, slept through it all – so he missed the publication. We were really pleased because we needed to sell every story for the money.

"Ross was a specialist mining journalist. I usually took the photographs, although I did both for some stories. We drove around in my 4-wheel drive, an old green Toyota LandCruiser. We had a fold-out camper trailer, so we could camp in any mining town. We had a lot of enjoyable experiences meeting a lot of interesting outback characters. At one time we did a shift on the 'grisly' in the Nepean nickel mine, half a kilometre underground, where rocks are smashed with a sledge hammer to make them go through a grill. That was a novel experience.

"I also wrote freelance photographic stories for the various Australian magazines, such as People magazine. If I saw something interesting, I'd photograph it, write a bit about it and find a sale for it. Those magazines were always good for petrol money."

Geoff with film crew on assignment for Lang Hancock's Australian Miner Newspaper

Geoff's nature shot:
The Paraburdoo Bungarra, locally known as 'Cecil', on tarmac.

On sports assignment for Lang Hancock's Sunday Independent newspaper

Hard at work for Lang Hancock's Australian Miner newspaper

"In the goldfields, we mostly wrote for mining newspapers, including mining magnate Lang Hancock's, Australian Miner newspaper. Ross was the editor. At one time when I was in Perth, Hancock was trying to expand his iron ore market to the cruel, despotic leader, Nicolae Ceausescu, the General Secretary of the Romanian Communist Party. For Hancock's paper, and for the State Government, I also photographed Ceausescu with premier Peter Dowding and Lang Hancock at Government House. While waiting for speeches I went downstairs to the basement area where refreshments were available for us, and there I sidled up to Ceausescu's guard detail, the most serious, stony-faced people I had ever met. They all looked depressed, old, faces lined and creased, like their working lives were not exactly joyful."

Adelaide

"Ross ended up coming back to Perth because his father was terminally ill, so I went on to Adelaide and got part time work there, writing for the ABC newsroom for some months. I also enjoyed writing propaganda stories for the Commonwealth Immigration Department. I photographed successful migrant families in their vineyards, with their big cars and houses conveniently framed behind them. These 'success stories' were published in European towns and cities to encourage immigration."

Geoff posing for a West Australian advertisement, 1967

"In Adelaide, I met a guy in a pub, Richard Ellis, who asked me if I'd like to run a news service in Alice Springs. I grabbed the opportunity with both hands and promptly drove there in my Toyota LandCruiser. As it happened, the office and living unit combined, was an old building in front of the town swimming pool. On my first night, after going to bed tired after my journey, I was disturbed by someone breaking in through the front door. The intruder was someone who knew the previous resident reporter and occasionally slept there. I told him to 'bugger off!' and fortunately, he never returned."

Land Rover and Chuck at Centralian office - Alice Springs 1972

Alice Springs Swimming Club conveniently adjoined to Centralian News office – 'Chuck' at the entrance, 1972

A town called Alice

"My new job in Alice Springs was to run the Centralian News Service. I had arrived in my Toyota LandCruiser, a short-wheel base 4WD. I later sold it and bought an aging long-wheel-base Land Rover which was going to be more reliable since the Toyota kept warping heads. I employed a signwriter to put the Centralian logo on the body and built in a drop-down bed in the back for distant assignments. I remember driving it around The Alice without a clutch – so much for reliability."

"The biggest news event ever happened there in 1972. I had just arrived back in Alice from the WA border, having escorted the Danish-born adventurer, Hans Tholstrup, who was riding a motorbike across Australia from Rockhampton to Perth in a record-breaking effort.

Then all hell broke loose ... I was stopped in the street and informed of a hijack in progress at the airport. Australia (notably Alice Springs) was in the midst of a rare high-jacking on a plane flying from Adelaide.

A male passenger, subsequently identified as a Czech migrant named Miloslav Hrabinec, had boarded the flight with a concealed sawn-off .22 ArmaLite rifle and a sheath knife strapped to his leg. After a long stand-off with police, after leaving the plane, the hijacker shot himself dead with his own rifle.

Wikipedia reports in more detail:

> *Hrabinec, the hijacker, then forced his way into the cockpit, however the captain informed him that he was unable to speak to him as he was too busy landing the plane. Hrabinec was informed that he needed to be seated for landing and he complied. After the plane landed, police commenced negotiations with him. According to accounts, Hrabinec stated his motive was not financial but that he wanted to commit suicide in a spectacular way by parachuting into a remote location and surviving for as long as he could before killing himself. To this end he demanded a light aircraft, a parachute and a jumpsuit. A civilian pilot and flying instructor, the local Aero Club manager, Ossie Watts, volunteered himself and his Cessna aircraft. An undercover police constable, Paul Sandeman, posing as Watts' navigator, was also on board the Cessna. According to Kaye Goreham, Hrabinec became*

suspicious upon seeing Sandeman and requested Goreham search Sandeman for weapons. Goreham did so but did not inform the hijacker when she felt a small firearm Sandeman had hidden. Goreham states that the policeman "went for his gun" and the hijacker shot Sandeman in the hand and stomach. Sandeman was also shot in the right shoulder and left arm. The hijacker ran off and Watts, who had been shown how to use a gun, minutes earlier, began shooting. Police marksmen also opened fire and Hrabinec was wounded. Hrabinec then retreated to a ditch where he fatally shot himself. Hrabinec was not identified as the hijacker until May 1973.

(https://en.wikipedia.org/wiki/Ansett_Australia_Flight_232)

"Meanwhile, back at my news office, whenever I attempted to phone the police or airport for updates about the hijack, a new voice would be on the line, desperate for news, blocking my own enquiries. The phone rang continuously, so I couldn't ring out to get the story. Roadblocks on the airport road also put a stop to news gathering. I later discovered that two Adelaide Advertiser office staff were tasked with getting through to me as a matter of urgency. The news organisations were hiring jets to get to Alice in a hurry to cover the story. This was the biggest news event of my life! I was a representative for many news organisations around Australia and experienced the extreme competition between rival journalists. When I convinced one reporter to share a picture-gram unit with a competitor, he nearly lost his job over it when his boss found out he was sharing resources.

Geoff single-handedly running the Centralian office in Alice Springs, 1971

"There was always something to report on in Alice Springs. Court cases that I dealt with included axe attacks, rapes and murders. There was also a lot of Aboriginal unrest and drunkenness and floods causing railway lines to wash away and threatening lives along the Todd River. There was outrage in Alice after people 'unknown' spray-painted the Devil's Marbles in bright reds, greens and blues. The Marbles are a natural set of huge boulders that are an Aboriginal sacred site. I also covered an air crash disaster north of Alice, when a twin-engine Beechcraft Baron crashed, with no survivors. I found and interviewed an American couple who had luckily missed the plane – they were very shaken up when I interviewed them.

Geoff surveying Alice Springs landscape, 1972

"Soon after my arrival, a dog I named 'Chuck the Wonder Dog' found me, so I adopted him. I later gave him more names based on two indigenous men who I met in town. One was named Sugar Diabetes, but in town he was called Frank Davis. The other was Titus Athenasius Retaranka. I traded cigarettes so they'd let me photograph them – not for publication – just for their striking photographic images.

Geoff training Chuck The Wonder Dog

"Having Chuck promoted a lot of social meetings with other people. I had a girlfriend, Vicky, who I met through Chuck when she said, 'Oh, what a lovely dog! Can I see where he lives?' (Geoff obliged.)

"It turned out she was a personal assistant to the Chief of Staff at the Hobart Mercury newspaper in Tasmania. While still in Alice Springs, this relationship prompted me to seek freelance work for this paper, in addition to the Launceston Examiner.

"During this time, I also freelanced for the Sydney Morning Herald, Melbourne Age, Brisbane Courier Mail, Adelaide Advertiser, Northern Territory News in Darwin and WA Newspapers in Perth. All reports were sent by 'reverse charge press telegrams', which were an extremely expensive form of transmission in the late 60s and early 70s (before personal computers and mobile phones). Also, I sent voice reports to 6PR radio station in Perth, 2GB in Sydney and 5AD in Adelaide. 5AD were always given reports first because they paid promptly, usually within two days."

Chapter Twenty One

More of Adelaide and Alice - and Therese

In 1973, Geoff took another trip from Alice to Adelaide for a brief holiday from the News Service, taking Chuck the Wonder Dog with him. One day, in the New South Wales bank in Adelaide, he met a woman named Therese, a medical student. They simply said 'hello' to each other and there was chemistry. They developed a fledgling relationship, and when Geoff returned to work in Alice, she soon visited him there.

"Our relationship continued for a year, or so, until we got married with a Catholic priest, who had to get permission from the bishop to marry us in an Adelaide park, instead of the church. I agreed to let our future children be Catholics, if they wanted to be. This was because Therese was Catholic, and someone had to marry us, and that's just what people did in the 70s. I went along with it because I'm just a push-over, really – and I always do what I'm told! I was attracted to Therese's good sense of humour, and we had some very funny times together."

Wedding: Therese and Geoff, with Chuck attending
Adelaide park, 1972

In Adelaide, Geoff traded his 4WD Land Rover for a Datsun 240Z sports car, an exciting, very popular little number! Soon, Geoff set off back to Alice Springs on the Ghan train, transporting the Datsun with him. In 1972, he resigned his outback reporter role with Centralian News Service and together with Therese – who flew up with Ansett – they drove back to Adelaide in the little yellow Datsun.

Stylish Geoff and Chuck with his Datsun 240Z, Adelaide 1972

"Some roads were really rough in those days. At one time, we were going too fast on the unsealed roads and bottomed out in a gully, resulting in a small hole in the petrol tank. While Therese held her finger over the leak, I carved twigs to fit. When we got to Coober Pedy, a mechanic suggested we put Velvet soap over it to seal it. That worked for a further six months before a proper repair. In the meantime, in Adelaide, I found employment as a reporter for Messenger Press, a suburban newspaper group."

And briefly owned VW Buggy – dogs guarding canoe

Geoff bought the VW Buggy as an extra vehicle more suited to outdoor adventure with his dogs. He sold it before leaving Adelaide but kept his canoe.

Chapter Twenty Two

Back to Perth

In 1975, the newly-wed couple decided to travel over the Nullarbor to Perth.

Crossing the Nullarbor, 1975

"Later I drove the Datsun to Perth, with Therese driving our Holden HD wagon, now with four dogs and a litter of pups … Within a week we were living in Dalkeith with Ross and Chris Louthean who had about three of their own Collie dogs – all the dogs stampeded together every time the postman delivered! Our extra canines included a rescue dog, which we named Nauseous, and two more adopted strays. One of them soon ran away, and another was given away, along with the puppies, leaving us with only two dogs in Perth, being the famous Chuck and Chunder!

Chuck pushing Chunder

Chuck loved a ladder!

Geoff back in WA visiting Robyn with Chuck, Chunder and Nausea Collie

"When I returned to Perth, I worked freelance for the Sunday Independent in Victoria Park, owned by Lang Hancock, which was in opposition to the West Australian Newspaper. This was my most frustrating job.

"One day, the journalists had a tip-off that some naked women were going to run out onto the cricket field at the WACA ground, and I arrived a bit too late, so I missed it. This was one of the biggest disappointments in my photographic career! Public nakedness was much more exciting in those early days."

Early 1970s: There's always time for sport

3rd place, annual Swan River 'Swim Through'

Training in canoe for first 'Avon Descent' challenge - competed with Keith Bensky in double kayak, coming 3rd in their class.

"On another occasion, I was working on a Saturday night taking photographs for either The West, or The Women's Weekly magazine, so I should have been out photographing an event. Instead, I dropped in on some friends and got them to dress up in their best outfits – minus their long pants – just photographing their top halves, and pretended they were at a ball. Those photos were published, and that tickled my sense of humour.

"In 1978, we had our first child, Brendan. Eighteen months later, our daughter, Emma arrived. Having babies was fulfilling, as I had always wanted children of my own. I loved kids. I used to admire other people's kids, and I felt ready for parenthood. In Alice Springs, I had loved watching people with their children, and yearned for that experience.

"When my own babies were born, being a light sleeper, I would be up and walking in an instant before I knew it, whenever they cried. I changed nappies and fed them. I washed the old cloth nappies and hung them out at night and, at that time, used safety pins. Later we moved on to disposable nappies. One scary memory is of Brendan, during a nappy change, when he flipped and became airborne, head first, but an instinctive grab by the ankle saved the day.

"Therese was a doctor. She went back to work within three weeks of Brendan's birth, so I looked after him. Eventually, when Emma was born, I had both of them at home with me while I was trying to manage my fledgling photography business. I had to entertain the kids while they were awake and then listen out for when they woke up from naps. I would give them a bottle each and get another hour's work done before preparing lunch."

Geoff worked from their large, modern home in Churchlands, Perth. It had a purpose-built office and darkroom and their three-car garage served well as a photographic studio.

Geoff, Jessie, Grandma Daisy & baby Brendan
Collie 1978

Chapter Twenty Three

Partnerships, Pools and Waters Beyond

"I created a business partnership with Joe Willner, a fellow cadet I befriended at the West Australian. I was there three weeks before Joe, so I knew everything!" – a contentious point of humour ... They soon became life-long friends.

(With permission) About their friendship, Joe wrote recently to Geoff:

> *Our 55 years of friendship started because you had a motorbike and were from Collie, two characteristics rarely found in Mt Lawley and because you started at 'The West' a week before me, you knew everything – or so I thought.*
>
> *We certainly didn't have religious belief in common but each respected the other, so here's one for Eve's book: Once, many moons ago, someone (one of the priests from Therese's church?) asked you what religion you followed – to which you replied that you were a Commercial Christian. When he asked what that meant, you answered on the spot that you went to church to make money!*
>
> *My dear late Mum also liked you very much and was thrilled that you came to Jerusalem for Sue's and my wedding. You've probably never forgotten my buck's*

night on the kibbutz. And who could forget the kookaburra imitations you sounded over Jerusalem from our flat every morning, not to mention the stir created by the wood carving of Jesus that you bought for Therese.

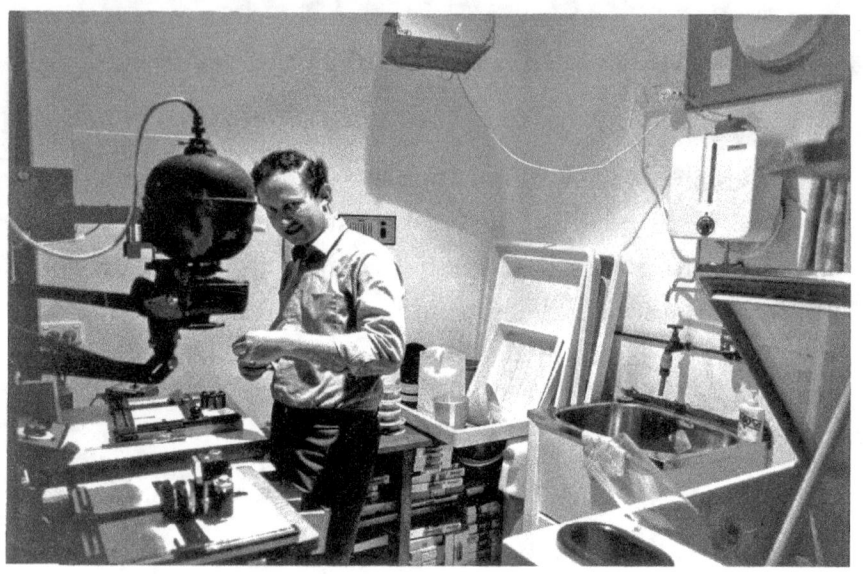

Joe working in black & white darkroom, Geoff's home/studio
Woodlands 1977

In their small photography business, they both took whatever photographic assignments they could get and shared their income from the business. Geoff recalls, "One day, Joe was delivering photo prints to Beatty Park swimming pool. It was a rainy day. He ran up the stairs and lost his footing, and went feet-first straight through a low window smashing all the glass – but he didn't get a scratch. We talk about that amazing event to this day when we get together.

"Beatty Park used to be managed by Rod Hounslow, with whom I was also good friends, and probably why I got in there for free for so many years! I also swam through the big holding tanks there, underground. In the mid 70s, I took my father to the pool to try out my aqualung which I had bought through the Sunday Times from an ex-SAS soldier. To make the experience more comfortable for Dad, Rod heated the pool up an extra couple of degrees, because it was winter. Dad thought that was pretty damn good."

Rotto infamy

"In 1968, I had an interesting experience to add to the rich tapestry of my life. I wasn't a great distance swimmer, but together with Wally Woodward, I set out to swim from Rottnest to Fremantle. Our boat dropped Wally and me off at the closest point to Perth. In the meantime, after we set off, the boat's engine flooded and they couldn't get it going. A strong current took us northwards. Consequently, our support crew couldn't find us. They were looking for us in the wrong area. Wally and I got tired of waiting for them, so we continued without them. An hour later, Wally got stung by a 'Man of War' when its big blue stinger tentacles trailed across his back, which I scraped off with my fingers. Later, he said that he almost walked on water because of the intense pain! At that point, we decided we should return to Rottnest. During this time, a 'lost at sea' alert had been put out for our rescue and both air and sea searches were initiated."

When the wayward swimmers had almost reached Phillip Rock, near the island, a Cessna aircraft flown with Geoff's press photographer friend, Kevin Davidson, was on board. He found them at the same time as a rescue boat. Geoff adds, "Kevin took pictures of us getting on board. Then we were taken to the nursing station on Rotto, where Wally was treated for serious stings. We made front page headlines in the Daily News in the summer of '68. The headline 'Bloody Idiots', quoting Rottnest Island manager, Ron Sullivan ... that was a bit embarrassing".

Geoff competed in the Perth to Rottnest swims and various Perth 'swim throughs' over the years. Initially, they were trend-setters before the official Perth-Rottnest event, which continues to this day.

Geoff continues: "In 1983, Shane McGurk, his cousin Brian, Peter Tanham and Craig Preshaw, were doing a Rotto to Perth swim, with me as support manager on the escort boat. Our borrowed police radios ran out of batteries, and there were too many swimmers for one escort boat. Shane got separated at one point and a small shark was seen swimming near him! However, when I attempted a solo long-distance ocean swim some time later, I suffered hypothermia which put a stop to my long solo swims. So, from then on, I swam in teams for the 18 km distance.

"The McGurks were a big part of our social life. I played hockey with Brian for many years. When we lived in Leederville, we invited the whole McGurk clan over for dinner and had a wonderful big barbecue together.

"In one of the first 'double crossings' organised, one Australia Day in the 80s, I helped a swimming and water polo friend, Peter Tanham, who asked me to help manage his swim. Peter was a very, very good distance swimmer, bike rider, and runner. My role in the crossing was to support and encourage Peter from the escort boat, but on nearing Rottnest, I jumped into the water and swam in front of him to encourage him during the final leg into Rotto. Peter said he would have given up otherwise, because the currents were so strong. He arrived at Rotto, got out of the water, had a cup of tea and a sandwich, recovered, and swam back to City

Beach – a thirty-six-kilometre round trip.

"For this event, Emma – who was just a little kid – had been persuaded to come on the escort boat to accompany me. I remember when at one stage, mid-voyage, Emma bravely jumped into the great dark water beside the boat to retrieve her drink bottle – quite a challenge for a little girl.

"Finally, we arrived at City Beach at dusk, instead of Cottesloe, due to the waves and a brisk sea breeze, just in time to see the Australia Day fireworks over the city. When we got close to shore, I swam the last little bit with Peter and ran up the beach with him. A photographer from the West Australian took a photo of us both, which amused me, because it looked like I had swum the whole distance with Peter. We returned to the escort boat to endure the long trek back to Fremantle up the Swan River to get home, making it a very long day.

"The Rotto swim is now a much bigger event, with local, interstate and international contestants of all ages. I remember the first time the long-distance swim became a publicly celebrated event, when Leslie Cherryman, now Leslie Meanie, did a successful solo crossing. Huge crowds waited on the North Mole in Fremantle and cheered her in as radio stations reported the event live."

Chapter Twenty Four

Men in Lycra

"I used to ride in a group known as 'Old Pappa's' because we'd meet and ride from Old Pappa's cafe in Fremantle. I did this five days a week for about a decade, mixing riding with swimming and water polo. Phillip Jenkins rode with us, and was known as 'The Legend'. I rode an Italian steel-framed racing bike by Tomassini that I had traded with Phillip for family photos.

"Riding was always a good fun, social event with lots of endorphins thrown in. We usually rode fifty to sixty kilometres before work, setting off at 5.30 am, riding alone to Fremantle – possibly picking someone up along the way – then having a coffee at Old Pappa's. My peloton set off at 6.20 am following the faster groups. Then we rode from Fremantle to Canning Bridge in Applecross, often adding a loop over the Mount Henry Bridge, across the Freeway almost to the city, back along Stirling Highway, left at UWA in Crawley and through to Dalkeith. Then it was back along Stirling Highway, and up the fire station hill – which was always exciting – down Eric Street in Cottesloe, left at Curtin Avenue, and back to Fremantle using the coast road, finishing back at Old Pappa's for another coffee ... 60 km later.

"After discussing life and the universe and solving world problems, we rode home. For me, that meant to Claremont, and later, to Mount Pleasant. As time moved on, I just went riding with a few of those friends, including Shane McGurk and Paul Malcolm.

"One day I did a longer ride (for me anyway) to South Fremantle, past Dorsogna Meats (which smells of pork and sausages), to Jandakot airport, then to the city and back to Fremantle. By the time I was close to home, I had travelled just over 100 kms and had to stop at a bike shop, where they gave me an electrolyte recovery snack because I was ready to collapse. I managed to get home, have a shower and throw myself on the bed, when I said a strong expletive as I realized I had to go to work … it wasn't surprising that I was a bit tired at work that day.

"I always felt joy when attacking hills, and on those days that I could keep up with the peloton, it was beautiful! Getting home exhausted was a good feeling too, except I still had work commitments."

Setting off to join the peloton

... and being farewelled by Bach, Mt Pleasant

Chapter Twenty Five

Destiny

Now, for more connections, let's return to that fateful original meeting on Christmas Day 1982, when Geoff crossed the threshold, from darkness to welcoming light!

Toni recalls, "This guy walked in, looking a bit troubled, a bit depressed, but my antennae stood up straight away."

Our Mum, Anne, a very intuitive person, was also never one to miss a handsome and talented man. While Toni was responding to this attractive man in the moment, Anne could see long-term potential, and wasted no time in encouraging a closer connection with her single daughter. The jolly atmosphere of the Christmas Day party was progressively helping Geoff to unwind into a happier, more receptive mood.

Anne actively corralled the couple with rhetorical questions like, 'Have you met my daughter? She's very creative you know!' With unwavering enthusiasm, she repeated variations on this theme. Being an artist herself, she knew Geoff would share her appreciation of creativity.

However, Toni soon reminded our mother that she had introduced her to Geoff at least three times, now unnecessary as sparks were already transmitting very well between the becoming-couple.

Toni enjoys recalling the day. "We were all drinking a lot

of champagne and some of us were smoking and having a good time. When we were handing out the presents, Geoff was lounging on the floor. Also, Ric commented that Geoff was one of the best photographers in Perth. As Ric is a very accomplished photographer himself, that was a good sign, as creative people are interesting to me. Geoff also had his own photographic business, so he seemed to me more like a capable, mature man than a boy. Perhaps his physical stature was important. He looked really good, tall, slim and very fit. He was a bit gaunt in the face, probably due to stress.

"But he also had a good sense of humour. I just couldn't handle a guy with no sense of humour. He was clever, and his humour was very surprising, coming out of left field. I was intrigued. While we were seated at the dining table, I couldn't believe how familiar he was, bumping knees with me under the table. Everything progressed very well.

"When it was time for Mum and I to go home at about midnight, as we were a long way from our homes, Geoff offered to drive us home in his V8 Statesman. So, we plopped Mum in the back seat, where she promptly fell asleep, and we drove her home. Then Geoff drove me home to Fremantle. I naturally asked him in for a coffee – and in the morning, Boxing Day, at about 8.00 am, Mum rang up to ask us to lunch. She loved entertaining, parties, cooking, men and people in general. She definitely wanted to encourage the relationship. She hadn't always been so enthusiastic about past partners. In her inimitable literary style, Mum exhorted me to 'Bind him in hoops of steel!' Meanwhile, Eve was reserving judgement on his suitability.

"During this time, I was working at the Fremantle Yacht Club as a barmaid and living in Little Howard Street in Fremantle. Geoff asked me to go with him to a Perth

Photographers' Association event. I said I couldn't go because I had to do a shift at work. Then I quickly arranged to swap shifts with another barmaid, but I didn't tell him at first, so that I wouldn't seem too much of a push-over!

"We went to an event at a photographic studio. It was a home movie starring John E. Porter, a Perth wedding photographer, dressed as Tarzan in a loincloth. It was hilarious. However, we couldn't keep our hands off each other, holding hands and kissing and annoying other people.

"A little later, I remember asking about four of my close friends to come to my place to meet Geoff. Optimistically, I had said, 'Come and meet the new man in my life!' All was well at the start when he was being actively friendly and funny …

…but after about an hour, he was falling asleep, sliding off his chair, almost under the table. I was so embarrassed, thinking my friends must be thinking 'Who's this character? Who's this hopeless person you've got together with?

"Geoff had a regular problem with tiredness at social gatherings, often falling asleep. Not only that, but I was a smoker, as were all of my friends and adult family. Geoff wasn't a smoker and never had been, although he had grown up with smokers all around him and had previously worked with smokers. I was diligent about brushing my teeth when with him, thinking it helped, but later he told me it didn't make any difference.

"I remember when I met Joe and Sue Willner for the first time at their home, I had to go out into the back garden to have a cigarette. When I came back inside, Joe said to Geoff, in front of me, 'I'm surprised you have got together with a smoker!' I felt very embarrassed and knew I had to stop."

Although Geoff never tried to make her feel guilty about her smoking, he eventually simply asked her to give it up. Toni responded with, 'If the Labor Party gets in at the next election, I'll give up.' It was 1982 and the election was about to happen. It was good news – the Labor Party won, with Bob Hawke as Prime Minister, and therefore, so did Geoff.

Of course, cigarette odour clings to a person's breath, hair and clothes. It is testament to the strength of his attraction, and tolerance, to put up with the smell and the smoky social atmosphere he often had to endure.

But Toni honoured her promise. "It wasn't easy, even though I had given up before for different periods of time, but Geoff's support made all the difference then. I had a few meltdowns in the process of giving up, but Geoff simply gave me hugs, calmed me, and encouraged me. It took me about six weeks to get through it all, knowing that if I even had one puff, Geoff would know."

Toni is still very grateful to Geoff for his unwavering support in the process for she has felt happier and healthier, being a committed non-smoker thereafter. Geoff has never allowed clients to smoke in his studios at any time, whether a general client, politician or other person of note, directing them outside if their need was too great. He even kicked Premier Brian Burke outside to have a smoke!

Toni reflects on Geoff's quirky behaviour relating to windows, recalling, "Once, early in our relationship, when I was visiting Mum, Geoff came to see me and arrived by climbing through the window, rather than by knocking on the door. He had a blue shirt on. His feet came through the window, and there he was! While there, I remember hugging him, and he responded warmly. I thought he probably hadn't been hugged for a long time. I liked the smell of him, the feel of him, and I loved his resonant, deep tone of voice. Whenever he rang me, which wasn't every day as I would have liked, and I heard his voice, my heart would do a revolution.

"I think he liked my sense of humour, my carefree attitude to things, my ability to adapt to change, my open-mindedness and my creativity. And, fortunately, I was available. Also, Geoff responded very well to Mum. He liked our family, and family has always been important to him."

Anne was an artist and a generally creative, open-minded, gregarious, strong and independent person. In fact, they shared these qualities, so they appreciated and understood each other in many ways. Geoff's easy, warm and confident interactions with Anne helped to strengthen Toni's positive view of him too. This view was enhanced when she learned how much he had loved his own mother.

Toni enjoying Geoff's dancing skills, and everything else …

Admittedly, we were all wrestling with his habit of falling asleep everywhere – which meant he was often 'not present' for periods at many social gatherings. In addition, in these early days, although we loved his humour, there were times we thought his humorous responses seemed rather excessive, making it hard to get to deeper, more meaningful levels. Yet, there were many bonding elements for Toni and the family. Not only was he handsome, fit, creative and capable, he was a distinct individual. He also cared about people and he had a passion for nature, beauty, colour, music and personal purpose, as our family did.

When Geoff entered the fold of our family, Anne had recently resumed playing classical piano, not having played since she was quite young – when she had worked up successfully through the classical music grades. Her passion for playing piano had been waylaid with marriage, career and other life events. She had largely and consistently expressed her creativity in art after marriage. At the time we met Geoff, she was in her late 60s and had started having individual lessons with a notable music professor at the University of WA, while also studying music history.

This shared affection for music cannot be underestimated in the union of our families ... in our common threads. A broad range of music had positively impacted all of our lives and lifestyles. Our father, Phillip, had a love of music too, mostly classical and folk, and apparently had attempted to learn the violin at one stage.

Concerning music, Geoff shares, "Around the time I got together with Toni, I still had a wooden recorder that had impressed me in primary school, so I played that every now and again. And I still have it. I also had a Jew's harp – an interesting, weird thing. You need a microphone to make it really 'go'. And I still had the harmonicas. Then I took possession of a piano accordion that Ross Louthean's Aunty Jean gave me, and I had some fun with that. She wasn't using it and I expressed interest because at many Italian and Greek weddings, bands with piano accordions provided the music, and I just loved listening to it."

If Geoff isn't playing an instrument at home, he and Toni are often listening to music. Geoff consistently listens to classical music while driving too.

Trials of a creative business

Toni recalls her initial involvement in Geoff's photographic studio. "One day, Geoff came to see me at the South Fremantle Yacht Club. I was thrilled and impressed by yet another 'surprise visit'! When he proposed that I leave that job to work with him, I jumped at it. Giving my notice was a real pleasure, and I soon went to work in his Napoleon Street studio in Cottesloe. Geoff welcomed some of my practical and aesthetic recommendations and my support.

"At that time, Joe Willner was doing the books for the studio. Everything was on file cards in those days. Geoff would often lose a card, or get things mixed up. Sometimes clients would come to the studio to collect their orders and the information could not be confirmed, causing some stress. He was often trying to do everything himself, everything necessary for the business. Tasks included photo shoots in the studio and on location, marketing, making appointments, showing images, ordering and picking up framed prints – but often doing the framing himself when required, late in the evening. Computers were not part of our world in the early to mid-1980s.

"He also used to do lots of weddings, often two or three weddings in one weekend, in eight to twelve hour stints. There was usually a photo shoot at the bride's home, continuing with the entourage on the way to the church, followed by the whole wedding event and the reception – waiting and photographing until everyone went home around midnight, or later. Throughout the wedding day, rolls of film had to be extracted carefully, new rolls loaded, while tripods and large light-reflectors had to be carried and moved around.

"Maintaining rapport with the bride's and groom's families was also paramount. For weddings, Geoff always had to plan, while also being spontaneous. He had to problem-solve throughout the whole process. I helped him with quite a few weddings, carrying equipment, holding and moving things for him, and I was exhausted!

"He had a passion to make the best images he could for the wedding couple and their party, and a determination that obstacles could be overcome.

"He was otherwise very organised, attending to every detail. At one time, due to the volume of work, someone suggested he get another photographer to do some of his photographic assignments, but he couldn't trust that he would get the professional result he required, so continued to do them himself. The energy output involved in these exercises was extraordinary at times, especially when it involved a fractious toddler, but his refusal to surrender was incredible.

"He's consistently great with kids. Parents always say they're amazed at how he manages to gain their children's trust, cleverly and humorously using psychology when needed. Some parents are able to be playful, but some just don't know how to fool around, being stiff and humourless when trying to control their kids. Geoff will do silly things like putting twigs on his head or barking like a dog to gain the children's trust and cooperation. At times, to improve the dynamic, he has even asked parents to step away or stop parenting for a minute!

"One of his clients once said to me, 'You can recognize a true master when they perform with such apparent ease and confidence'. But Geoff has never betrayed how much effort it takes to achieve his goals, all in good time with good humour. However, a depleted supply of energy after work sometimes resulted in a short fuse at home, and sometimes a lack of emotional 'availability'."

Toni adds, "Then he would get up very early to go swimming with his mates. They were training up to do the Rottnest swims but he also went cycling, played hockey and water polo. It cut into other things in life. In the lifestyle mix, his time and energy were regularly spent before work! I thought he'd got into a habit, although I knew it had always been a huge, important part of his life. Still, it was also a lifelong pattern of 'escape'. And I had a very different circadian rhythm."

Progressing the relationship

After about three months of spending time together, Geoff said to Toni one day, "So, how would you like to move in?" Toni was excited about taking the next step, while at the same time, being a little cautious. But Geoff always talked positively about the future, so she soon moved into his Davies Road, Claremont villa unit, and enjoyed settling in as his partner. Then, one day, he said, "If you want to have kids, you'll have to find someone else, because I've been there and done that." Toni felt disappointed and she considered it an unrealistic thing to say, because as she says, "... a person doesn't normally just go out and find someone to have a child with," but she understood his position.

However, one evening around Christmas in 1983 at the Jade Court restaurant in Cottesloe, while sharing Wolfblass Rhine Reisling and a meal, Geoff asked Toni, "Would you like to have a baby?"

Toni comments, "I thought he was absolutely wonderful with his own children, although I often had the kids when he was at work and I didn't think I'd signed up for that. During the times that Geoff had the children from his first marriage regularly stay with us, his work demands meant that I had to look after them alone in the part-time co-parenting arrangement.

"I remember that Emma told Geoff early in the piece, 'She isn't the right one!' I had mixed feelings about Therese and knew there was a lot of unresolved stuff there. Geoff often arranged for his kids to stay, but didn't always tell me – when the kids didn't want to be with me, just wanting their mother. Emma would look at me with daggers after Therese dropped them off. I accepted that I was not Brendan and Emma's mother and that the co-parenting had to be worked out between Geoff and Therese. It was often tense and awkward between Therese and myself.

"Fortunately, Geoff was wonderful the way he played with the kids, and they adored him. He could play the best games with them. It came naturally to him."

Geoff recalls, "Emma was gregarious and outgoing as a young child, while Brendan was more insular and introverted. I remember asking Brendan at about three or four years old, why he preferred to just play with his Masters of the Universe, rather than play with others, and he replied without looking up, 'I like diving into my little pool of fantasy.' Another time he was transfixed, watching something, saying in his own special way that they were 'disappearing and then s'appearing again."

When Toni and Geoff found out they were pregnant, they promptly arranged a champagne party at the studio to celebrate with a couple of friends.

Toni reflects, "In those days, there were no warnings about drinking alcohol when pregnant. However, fortunately, morning sickness quickly kicked in and alcohol lost its appeal. Geoff was very supportive and lovely about our pregnancy. He even dreamt that he had a baby himself, at the time, and that it was in all the newspapers!"

Geoff explained, "My main concern in the dream was about who would get the Australian rights to publish – maybe the Women's Weekly, or even world rights could be granted. The overriding theme was that there was no hanky-panky involved in this pregnancy – it just happened because I loved kids."

Toni continues, "Having Jasmine was wonderful. The birth took a very long twenty-seven hours, starting from contractions at home in Davies Road, Claremont, but with most time spent in King Edward Maternity Hospital in Subiaco. So, she was born on 3rd June, 1983. Nitrous Oxide was encouraged for pain relief, but it didn't suit me and I refused it. Geoff stayed the whole time with me. Because the birth took so long, Jasmine was a bit blue, but she picked up very well. She was 9lbs 2ozs. Geoff was very happy and took some wonderful black and white photos in the hospital, and later on in the studio.

"When I had to feed Jasmine in the middle of the night, Geoff often got up to sit with me to keep me company. Although Geoff had always cared for Brendan and Emma during the night, once I had Jasmine, I naturally got up to attend to all the children. My circadian rhythms, previously 'out of synch' with Geoff's early risings, changed to better match his. In the 80s, the father's surname was automatically given to the children, without question, so Geoff would say 'Jasmine Fisher' all the time and I felt a bit sidelined, until I asked, 'Do you ever think about getting married?' to which Geoff replied, 'I think about it every second day!' So, we decided on the date of 31st December of that year, 1984."

It was also just over one year since they met, and they thought a naturally combined New Year's Eve party and wedding would be perfect for the celebration, a double-party. They are both Leos, after all! I also muse over the significance of New Year's Eve, thinking about Henry's arrival in Fremantle as a boy, entering his own new phase of life.

Chapter Twenty Six

The wedding – and family

Completing a cycle, the wedding was held at their original meeting place, at Ric Syme's home, and his mother, June, offered to be their celebrant. Toni and Geoff bought modest, attractive wedding rings and new outfits for the wedding ceremony. They both looked gorgeous and were extremely happy. The wedding ceremony was conducted in perfect weather in the home's lovely garden.

The groom and bride with near-7-month-old Jasmine wearing baby's breath halo, 1984

Geoff with little Brendan and Emma

Geoff celebrating with Robyn and Janis

Geoff's sister, Janis, with her husband Bert, made the long trip from Hawaii to join them all. The house was decorated everywhere with flowers and countless large, white candles which provided abundant warm, atmospheric light. Caterers provided a stream of exquisite, tasty hors d'oeuvres, while champagne and other beverages flowed all night.

Everyone danced madly, enjoying the music and communing over several hours, all declaring later that it was the greatest, happiest party in their memory. Toni and Geoff took Jasmine with them to a Perth hotel for their honeymoon night, having pre-ordered a cot for her. Toni comments, "When we arrived in our room, we found a bottle of MUMM Champagne from Therese. We thought this was really magnanimous."

Joe and Sue Willner visiting the happy honeymooners next morning at Sheraton hotel

Kids

In time, the blended Fisher family expanded with the birth of a fourth child – Toni's second. Their son, Ashley, was born on 24th August, 1987, in the lounge room of their home at 24 Webster Street in Nedlands with the professional, caring assistance of a lovely midwife, Tamsin Murphy.

Toni recalls, "We were ready to go to King Edward Hospital nearby if any complications arose, but this birth took only five hours. It coincided with a corporate photo shoot at the studio. When Geoff got that important call, he had to get his studio colleague, Martin Davidson, to take over the shoot. He rushed home in good time. Ashley weighed exactly 10 lbs, as healthy as could be. He had the same birth weight as Geoff."

Just as Ashley was being born, Anne was unloading party food and drink from her car outside. Then Geoff called me, and a couple of close friends including Heather Grauaug with her young daughter, Alex, and studio manager, Deanne Marsden. During the labour, Heather had been babysitting Jasmine, so she brought her home at the right time too. As planned, everyone arrived to celebrate in the lounge room with party food and champagne, and Geoff videoed the event.

Three-year-old Jasmine was always involved in the pregnancy and impending birth, and was encouraged to help give Ashley his first gentle, welcoming bath in the lounge room. Toni fondly remembers, "He was such a good-looking, calm, lovely baby, just as Jasmine was. We quickly presented Jasmine with a generous gift from Ashley – a lovely little doll's stroller to push her own 'baby' around in. She accepted the gift with delight and was very happy to meet her brother.

Jasmine surprised by Ashley's cry, 1987

Jasmine, Emma and Brendan at the birth of baby Ashley at Webster Street, Nedlands, 1987

"However, during Ashley's first week out in the world, he caught a cold and was given antibiotics. He also had a chest x-ray at the hospital, so that was really unfortunate, being such a young baby."

Emma and Brendan shared homes with both parents, with many adjustments required. By the time Ashley arrived, they had already accepted Jasmine, and Toni as their father's new wife. The evolving Fisher family lived in Webster Street between 1984 and 1992, a home the children remember with great affection and nostalgia. Life was very social, musical and fun.

Flautists Brendan and Geoff with family and friends,
Webster St, Nedlands, 1989

Classical practice: Geoff on flute, mother-in-law Anne on piano,
Jasmine on recorder, Webster Street, Nedlands home, 1990

Dress-ups

Jasmine and Ashley having a fun birthday

Brendan and Emma grew up much of their time with Jasmine and Ashley. They usually interacted and played together very happily, although occasionally some jealousies crept in.

Toni recalls, "In the beginning, Emma had mixed feelings, hugging Jasmine one minute and slapping or pushing her away the next. She could also enjoy pushing Jasmine a little too high on the swing at times! In the early years, Emma showed the most difficulty with her emotions in the new family mix, having frequent nightmares, when Geoff always attended to her and calmed her. And once, when Therese visited the family at our Webster Street home, Jasmine happily climbed up onto Therese's lap, and Emma reacted with a full meltdown."

In time, affection, patience, family fun and holidays helped the children to blend. Geoff's propensity to use 'reverse psychology' frequently worked wonders to dissolve children's complaints into laughter – it's very hard to keep complaining when surprisingly coerced into laughter! And, Geoff and Toni consistently took photos and videos of all of them, creating opportunities for further interaction and fun – and for memories later.

Geoff, Emma, Jasmine – Cottesloe, 1980s

Country holiday - cooking on wood stove:
Emma and Jasmine, Toni and Brendan

Mother-in-law, Anne, encouraging little Jasmine to sketch,
Kalbarri family holiday, 1986

From around 1990, Geoff and Toni made friends with Philomena ('Phil') Kjellgren – now Gilmour - and her two daughters, Alannah and Libby, who attended Beehive Montessori primary school. Jasmine and Ashley also started their education there and the two families met and melded very happily with a car-pool arrangement.

As Geoff says, "Our families had a lot of fun together in the 1990s. When we'd say goodbye to our kids in the morning, we'd sometimes not see them until the next day because Phil would take them home to stay with her kids until the next day. We'd have her kids sleep over too. And, if Ashley was ever misbehaving, Phil would threaten him with another night at her place, and we'd all fall about laughing, knowing he'd really have a great time there. The threat worked – he would behave himself – because Phil was so kind ... but strict.

"Contrasting Phil's strict manner, I used to put all the kids in the trailer and drive slowly over the curbs between Nedlands and Dalkeith to give them the equivalent of a Royal Show experience, only stopping if one of them dared to stand up – quite illegal, of course – in line with our reckless, permissive but fun parenting! I spoilt Libby at times, giving her piggy backs and 'swingies' because she was born with a serious heart defect. Sadly, she died at eight years of age, long before her time. We were all affected, and we were particularly concerned at the time about the impact it had on Jasmine.

"However, while we were all enjoying our times together, Friday nights at our Nedlands home were 'concert nights', centred around our large wooden coffee table, when all the kids would provide spontaneous performances while the parents drank a lot of bubbly and prepared late meals, enjoying the festivities. There was always a varied collection of kids, but they often included Phil's two girls and Ray Constantine's two, Ryan and Sarah, as well as Jasmine's good friend Selina. We had great family holidays with Phil, and also with Ray. In addition, Phil later had the best divorce party ever at my O'Beirne Street studio!"

Chapter Twenty Seven

Revisiting Collie

Toni fondly recalls family visits to Collie. "We all went to Collie often, to visit Robyn, her husband and their children, Timothy, Quito and Chrishelle, who lived in the old family home in Ogden Street. When all the cousins got together, they were like a wild herd of animals running from one end of the house to the other, some still learning to walk, with the older ones helping them and including them in their games and play. The old flywire door at the back was constantly slamming as they rushed out to the garden. We loved to see and hear that. All the kids revelled in the natural environment there. Robyn also kept lots of dress-up outfits for the children to play with, so they were always entertained. There were no video games, iPads, computers or mobile phones in those days.

"The Ogden Street home was still very much as it was when Henry and Jessie had lived there – still with the roof ladder Geoff used with Henry, trimmed privets outside, red Laminex kitchen table, leadlights and solid jarrah floorboards inside, with many other old, inner and outer features remaining. The gardens were still flourishing, as well as the chooks."

24 Ogden Street - with roof ladder before brick garage was built. Collie

Toni with Jasmine on a typical foggy, frosty morning,
24 Ogden St backyard. Collie c.1984

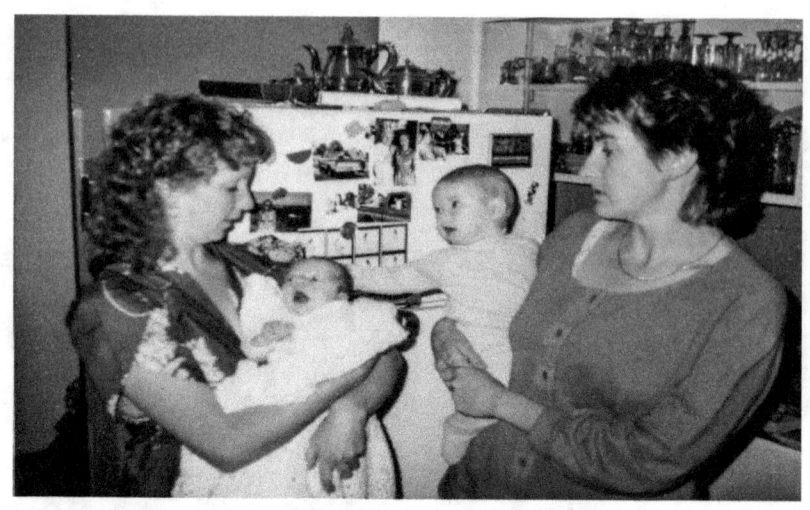

Robyn and Toni with babes in arms,
Ogden Street, Collie, 1984

"It was always fun to spend time with Robyn. I could share my mothering role with her, as we both had babies and toddlers at the same time, and motherhood involved a lot of sewing for us both."

Around this time, when the children were very little, Toni was deeply touched when Geoff bought her a top-of-the-range Pfaff sewing machine with a Horne sewing cabinet to house it, a very welcomed surprise Christmas gift. "I remember how fondly Geoff watched me sew with it, and I realized that his own mother, Jessie, sewed a great deal for him and the family.

"In addition, Robyn was a barmaid in Collie, so we shared that experience too. Even at that time, there was very little to see in Collie – just the service station, hardware shop, the draper's and the pub. Sometimes it was very hot and, having no air conditioning, we would go for a swim in the Blue Lake, created out of a disused open pit mine where Geoff used to swim as a kid.

Geoff also recalls, "It was always interesting visiting the old home with so many things to rediscover, such as a big cross-saw with large teeth and a handle on each end, in the back shed. It was the kind that required two men to use it, like the timber fellers used. Alan had done a coloured chalk drawing on it in about 1956. Robyn's son, Quito, still has it. And there was still a hole in the sleepout window where John Surasky, from next door, had shot a pellet through it while playing. This reminds me of a similar incident in which I smashed a neighbour's window with a rock missile, propelled with a 'shang-hai' or 'ging', something I never owned up to.

"And going back revealed the disappearance of the two picture theatres I grew up with, the location of one of them having become a shopping centre. Houses had become more up-market, with fewer made of weatherboards. And one set of traffic lights had been installed in the main street, which was a shame."

Later, Robyn moved to Perth and the Fisher clan were able to interact and support each other more often. The old Collie house was sold, and for Geoff, further trips to Collie have become rare, except for funerals. The house still stands at 24 Ogden Street, much as it was.

Chapter Twenty Eight

Studio changes

Naturally, life moved on. The blended Fisher family were a unit. Geoff had moved from his Napoleon Street studio, next setting up in Gugeri Street, Claremont, followed by O'Beirne Street where Toni worked as an employee with Geoff for some years, together with other staff.

Geoff and Toni, O'Beirne Street studio, Claremont, 1990

In 1990, having relocated to the attractive nearby studio in O'Beirne Street, Geoff employed a 'lovely English rose' named Helen Large to work at the studio with his sister Robyn. Together they dealt with clients' enquiries and appointments, showing photos for selection and sales, filing negatives, invoicing and other duties. The female duo were very compatible throughout the ten years they worked together for Geoff, and he was grateful to have them both working for him. Like Robyn, Helen was an excellent employee, being lively, humorous, tolerant, and very capable.

Toni shares, "Before Helen was employed, I had been very concerned about a series of Geoff's unsuitable employees, and spoke about it to our mother, Anne. Then, following her advice, we put out a newspaper advertisement requesting written applications for the position. After we deleted the clearly unsuitable applicants, we took the possible candidates' handwritten applications to Mum to analyse, as her repertoire of professional skills as a clinical psychologist included graphology. She said that Helen was the one and only, an eminently suitable applicant for our needs. And Helen proved her right. We were so grateful to Mum for that. Helen later became Helen Adshead when she married journalist and television news reporter, Gary Adshead, who proposed to her in the studio, on bended knee – so it was party time, yet again."

While working at the studio, Toni tried her hand at photography herself, with Geoff's mentorship, and even won an award for a portrait photograph of Helen. The award was presented by the famous photographer, Lord Litchfield, who was visiting from overseas and attending the Perth Photographers' Association awards night that year. However, she soon decided that there was only enough room in their relationship for one photographer, and that was clearly Geoff. Fortunately, she had plenty of other creative interests available to her, but she assisted when needed. She and Gary, with their two sons, Ben and Harrison, maintain a strong friendship with them all to this day … although she is known to still joke, "I gave Geoff the best ten years of my life!"

Helen and Gary Adshead catching up with Geoff and Toni
Attadale, 2022

Helen, Toni, Eve, Geoff, Gary and Robyn

In 1987, Geoff received a Master of Photography Silver Award by the Australian Institute of Professional Photographers (AIPP) for his portrait below:

Jasmine

Geoff enjoyed his time in the AIPP, as it provided a range of stimulating opportunities to challenge himself, to share and learn with passionate colleagues, including good friend Ric Syme, and to support other emerging photographers.

While at the O'Beirne studio in 1997, Geoff won a portrait competition with NuLab in Melbourne.

Nulab's Nulook Festival award 1997: 'Overall Prize for Portrait' section

Geoff adds, "John Dowell and his wife Sandra are our long-time friends who used to run NuLab in Melbourne. Through the years, we have been able to get together in Perth and stay with their family in Melbourne at different times. They came over for my 70th as a lovely surprise and now we are jokingly competing for the greatest number of grandchildren."

More Music

Interwoven through business and home life, Geoff has always continued his music interests, commenting, "One New Year's Eve, I went to Zenith music store in Claremont and came home with a saxophone and a piano. At some earlier stage, I had also bought a flute and had music lessons with a Polish teacher who was a member of the West Australian Symphony Orchestra. I enjoyed the flute the most. Eventually I decided the piano had to go, and I sold the saxophone.

"Also, at one point in the mid 1990s, a good friend, Ray Constantine, was learning flute and saxophone and he invited me to join a band that practised once a week in his photographic laboratory called Copy Chrome. The band leader, Rex Jordan, had an amazing array of instruments which he lent to band members. He lent me a bass saxophone to play in the band, and that was very enjoyable. Somehow, we even found ourselves playing for aged care home residents a couple of times, and I think someone complained that we were out of tune on one occasion. Anyway, that bass saxophone had an absolutely beautiful sound, but eventually I gave it back, and the band faded out. Sometime around then, I purchased the electric piano that I have now. It's got a full-size keyboard."

Geoff and Ray still in synch, 2022

Chapter Twenty Nine

A scare at home

When the Fishers were living in Kingsway in Nedlands, Jasmine was nearly three years old and Toni almost five months pregnant. Then, one warm, cloudy day, with Geoff at work, Toni was busy washing breakfast dishes and cleaning up the kitchen with Jasmine at home. For some time, Toni was cleaning around the sink and benches, set below a large window overlooking the backyard where Jasmine was happily playing with the young children from next door. Suddenly, two of the children appeared next to Toni, telling her that they couldn't find Jasmine, saying that she had '... chased a little doggie and fell into a pool', but Toni didn't know about any pool nearby. She questioned them further, but couldn't understand them very well, and with rising anxiety, asked them to show her where they had been playing and where they thought Jasmine had gone.

"They led me across the road, past an overgrown brick fence, then through a rusty gate, to reveal a swimming pool with a plastic cover over its surface. When I saw the pool, I asked the children, "Where is she?" They said they didn't know! So I pulled the cover back and, horrified, saw little Jasmine floating just under the cover, her body in a vertical position with her arms spread out. Immediately, I jumped into the pool, still wearing my denim pregnancy smock and shoes, and threw Jasmine out onto the poolside, just as I briefly sank below the surface of that awful dark, mossy water. When Jasmine hit the side, she made noises and started crying, so I knew she was alive and breathing.

"Amazingly, Jasmine didn't seem to have swallowed any water and appeared physically alright. I took her home, checked her all over again, showered and dressed her warmly, and cuddled her as much as I could, feeling tearful as the possibility of a dire outcome weighed on me. I was concerned that Jasmine had been in contaminated water and watched for signs of ill-health. I quickly rang Geoff, and then the hospital to check whether Jasmine should go to emergency, but they said that as she did not seem to be suffering physical effects, we shouldn't worry, to simply observe her. They also said that it was common for submerged children to hold their breath automatically, preventing immediate drowning, especially when they hit cold water. I thought Jasmine must have been submerged for two or three minutes."

When Geoff was told, he was also upset. He felt very emotional to think they could have lost her. A day or two after this event, one early morning, I remember visiting them all, only to see Geoff with Jasmine, before going to work, sitting on one of her little wooden chairs at her little table, his knees squeezed up high at his chest, as they quietly ate their breakfast cereal together.

Jasmine seemed to be emotionally sound, as she continued to be the bright, sociable little girl she had always been. Yet Toni and Geoff recognised that the incident must have been a shock for her, and that she may not have been able to communicate deeper, unconscious feelings. They kept her near, but did not inhibit her play. Water was always an important feature of the family's lifestyle too, so she was soon taken to swimming lessons at Kevin Duff's swimming school.

3-year-old Jasmine's swimming lesson

Chapter Thirty

Medical relationships

It is worth noting that Geoff seemed to progressively manifest family and close friends from the medical world throughout his adult life. So, in 1990, when Toni told Geoff about her desire to study to become a naturopath, he naturally said: "If you want to do that, I'll support you." Soon Toni began her naturopathic course, following a long-held ambition to work in natural health and medicine. One contributing factor was that, before she became pregnant with Ashley, she had sadly miscarried twins at a very early stage. Both she and Geoff were very upset and grieved their loss. Toni soon sought treatment from a prominent naturopath who prescribed an appropriate herbal remedy and shortly afterward, a very healthy pregnancy occurred, resulting in their welcome baby boy, Ashley.

Much earlier in life, Toni had been a psychiatric nurse at Heathcote Mental Hospital, and our sister Leith had also done some training to be a nurse in her earlier life, before taking up architecture. Our father, Philip Creed, was a general practitioner and later on, also an anaesthetist. One of his two surgeries was designed and built into our home in North Beach. Even as a child, Toni liked to go secretly into the surgery to find ways of treating cuts and abrasions on herself, but at times, she also 'persuaded' her friends to be painted with mercurochrome and bandaged in the surgery, in our father's absence!

In addition, a great number of our close relatives are highly qualified medicos or work in medically-related occupations. Our mother, Anne, was a clinical psychologist with a great deal of knowledge about medicine. I have also trained in kinesiology and reflexology, so Toni and I have gainfully shared our nutritional, biochemical and energetic knowledge and interests – and Geoff has benefitted from both our skills. Traditional and allied medicine is a fundamental part of many of our relatives' occupational culture and knowledge base. Geoff's daughter, Emma, is a highly trained kinesiologist now too. Synchronistically, Geoff initially married a doctor, and since then has made many close friendships with medicos, some within his sporting life … all highly relevant to his story … so, more weaving and wafting of threads!

Geoff supported Toni in practical ways throughout her studies, helping her to furnish and equip her clinic rooms. At times she worked in shared clinics and at other times from home. For some time, she worked at the University of WA Child Care Centre as a cook to help pay for her fees, applying her nutritional and culinary skills to the task successfully. Geoff believed in her study mission and was proud of her.

Unfortunately, although Toni was dedicated, passionate and extremely competent, she found it very difficult to get enough financial reward from clinic practice. Her grateful clients had very positive outcomes, but that alone could not financially sustain her business – a common problem for creatively-minded, care-focused natural health practitioners. Admittedly, Toni was inclined to be over-generous to clients with her time and energy. She finally made the difficult decision to retire, but her personal interest and commitment to keep learning has never ceased. It is part of who she is, and her knowledge has been invaluable for the whole family.

Chapter Thirty One

Optimism

Toni has always loved the fact that Geoff can fix things, partly because our father could not – and did not try. (However, as children, we may have failed to fully acknowledge his talent for expertly fixing people, as a doctor!) Toni believes Geoff expresses his intelligence this way, meeting a challenge with creative ingenuity, adaptability and perseverance, as he does with his photography. He may have never encountered a task before, but that just inspires his curiosity.

In July 2001, our sister Leith Conybeare, together with her husband Darrel, invited Toni and Geoff to attend her 60th birthday, staying at a house on the estuary at Pittwater, near Sydney. Relating to this event was that Leith had mentioned that, while she appreciated Geoff's creative occupation as a photographer and his good sense of humour, she was a little surprised that Toni hadn't chosen a partner with an academic background, given her own university studies. Living on the other side of the country, Leith and Darrel had not had much opportunity to really get to know him, or to see him in partnership with Toni.

However, at one stage during the visit, the birthday group had to get from a boat onto a little jetty below a long set of steps leading to the house. While negotiating the process,

Leith dropped her keys in the water. Geoff immediately ripped off his jeans and jumped into the water wearing only his jocks, quickly rising to the surface to present the rescued keys to Leith. Toni thought Leith was impressed by his prompt, helpful response to the situation, not to mention his impressive physique! Over ensuing years, Geoff and Toni enjoyed other enjoyable trips to Sydney to see them.

Leith and Darrel also enjoyed trips to Perth, usually staying with Toni and Geoff, and always contributing to their party gatherings. Leith has invariably shared her sophisticated, funny yarns, all with clever twist-punchlines, frequently matched by friend Heather Grauaug's yarns. Geoff and Robyn's own brand of Fisher humour always enters the mix too, so wit and laughter have flowed through both sides of the family and friends, sparking our relationships, bonding us all.

At one time, when Toni was studying sculpture and drawing at Claremont Art School, Geoff made generous contributions to her work by photographing them in unusual ways. In one instance, with waves breaking on the shore, he shot images of a nude Toni, wearing her wire fish sculpture construction. Her tutor was ecstatic and praised the result as 'performance art'! In addition to that, during this course, Toni became pregnant and could no longer fulfil the requirements of the course, as sculpture in particular can be quite physically demanding. Toni recalls, "Geoff just took over the course. He completed the year for me. I was impressed how someone who had had no formal training in perspective drawing, for example, could make such accomplished sketches."

Concerning optimism, Toni remembers going with him to assist at a wedding when it started to rain. "The upset wedding party complained, saying: 'Oh, no, it's all ruined!'

Then I witnessed how he could turn disadvantage into advantage. Geoff promptly pulled some very large, rainbow-coloured photographer umbrellas from the car boot and turned the headlights on at just the right angle. The lights, beaming through the darkness, created wonderful evocative images. He set the tone, transformed the experience for everyone, and produced beautiful photographs of the occasion that were greatly appreciated."

Stresses

One of Geoff's male friends once described him as 'a compulsive optimist' – clearly a two-sided sword, and Toni adds, "The less favourable side of the sword sometimes manifests as a lack of preparedness for things to *not* work out in life, with a tendency to forget the problems, having impulsive mishaps, with some errors of judgement. He is the quintessential example of someone living in the moment, but who is not the Dalai Lama!

"Being in the moment can sometimes express itself in reactive outbursts too. Sometimes Geoff lost his temper when we lived in Webster Street in Nedlands. One time, he came home in the evening, walking in the front door with a bag of Smarties and, unthinking, was about to give all of them to just one of the children. When the other three protested, he said, 'You don't all have to have the same!' I argued with him about it, so he threw them all across the room, which excited the kids and, delighted, they all scrambled madly for them. That gave us a good laugh and transformed the mood completely.

"On another occasion, Geoff got home after work rather stressed, and announced to everybody: 'Too much TV! I'm going to cut the cord off the back of it.' Usually, he just pulled the cord out of the wall socket, but one day he chopped it off. Then he hid it. The kids asked, 'Where's the TV?' and he said, 'It's at the repair shop.' The television reappeared when Geoff decided he wanted it back there, but it was removed intermittently."

This caused considerable stress for the children. Toni believes the television created too much visual and auditory distraction for him when there was too much going on in his head, with work stress and tiredness at the end of the day. At the same time, he was often drawn to watch it intensively if it was there. He could not manage his time and attention around television in a consistent, balanced way.

As Toni says, "Geoff gets distracted easily anyway – so sometimes the TV issue was like the kettle boiling over. And apart from that, he also frequently complained about the standard of my housework performance when he came home after work, even when I was also working. But he refrained from doing any housework himself."

My own observations were that in those days, Geoff was also capable of saying outrageous things to Toni about the state of the house when he arrived home. She often felt very hurt by this. At times, as a witness, I was shocked at his outbursts which seemed illogical and out of proportion to me, given that Toni had little children to care for, plus cooking, cleaning and many other tasks. No doubt, her housekeeping skills and dedication did not match Geoff's mother's standard. There were times when Toni sought some 'professional', impartial advice from our mother, Anne, which helped a great deal. Gradually, she learned to stand up for herself more with Geoff – and has steadily gone from strength to strength!

Over the years, they undertook some significant formal psychotherapy, separately and together, which helped a great deal too. But their common, natural ability to let things go, when reasonable, and their living-in-the-moment way of being, has kept their partnership strong. As Toni comments, "Arguments were created, but they often passed as quickly as they occurred."

Geoff's work has often made huge demands on his time and energy, but he has always enjoyed his photographic relationship with clients and the creative challenge of making great images for them. Yet, the administration, accounting and management of his studio business has often caused stress, particularly at intense, pressured times like Christmas. It has often been said that very creative people need managers for their business. Typically, Geoff could get so involved in his creative work that he would not attend to a lot of other administrative detail – sometimes even forgetting appointments, although often saved by attentive staff, particularly Robyn, or Toni, very aware of his propensity to distraction. For Geoff, however, the stress produced in such situations could erupt in ways that didn't seem fair or logical to staff or family.

Sport was his way to relieve stress. However, his sport took more of his time before or after work, and more of his total energy in a day, which frustrated Toni, and had consequences. She often urged him to reflect on his negative stress and to try to balance his lifestyle in order to be more 'available' to himself and his family.

Nevertheless, she appreciated that he needed to have sport in his life, understanding that such activity released endorphins and oxytocin making him feel strong and happy, as well as keeping him fit. She also recognised the high social importance of sport which allows competition and camaraderie with a wide circle of friends. She could see how Geoff actively encouraged his children to enjoy healthy, physical activity in a wide variety of beneficial ways that usually involved connection with nature and the outdoors.

Taking two-year-old Ashley for a gentle ride, 1989

(L to R) Emma, Ashley, Toni, Geoff, Bach, Jasmine, Brendan
Swanbourne Beach c.1994/95

(L to R) - Brendan, Jasmine, Emma, Ashley with Geoff and Toni
Cottesloe c.1997

Fisher family, Cottesloe c.1995

Chapter Thirty Two

The joy of travel

Geoff and Toni's first overseas holiday as a couple was to Greece in 1985 with fourteen-month-old Jasmine.

Toni reflects, "Beforehand, some friends commented that it was a brave thing to do with such a young toddler, but in fact, the Greek people were warmly drawn to Jasmine and it was a definite social advantage to have taken her. They naturally adore children, but Jasmine was also very sweet with her blonde hair and the face of an angel. She was always happy, smiling, calm and curious. She would stretch out her little arms to friendly strangers, and because of her, we were sometimes invited from the street by different women into their homes. We were given so much warm hospitality. People were drawn to Jasmine in restaurants too, so we were able to meet lots of lovely people. However, because she constantly wanted to engage with everybody there, once or twice we had to tie a string to her ankle, connected to the leg of our table, to manage her happy interactions."

Some overseas travel was possible as a result of Geoff's participation in the Masters Water Polo team. Both Geoff and Toni were able to take a treasured trip to Italy for international competitions in 2004.

Intrepid travellers with toddler Jasmine in Greece, 1985

Geoff competing in Italy with the Perth Masters water polo team. 2004

In spite of anxious, 'white-knuckled' driving required on the Autostrada in Italy, the rest of their experience was close to heaven as they soaked up the lively Italian spirit of friendship and hospitality offered to them everywhere. The team did not win overall, but the joy of the trip was far more valuable to them.

Toni had studied Italian in her Bachelor studies at university and Geoff was able to draw on a few expressions he had learnt in his early life with friends and neighbours in Collie, as well as during various work experiences. While staying in a hotel in Riccioni on the east coast of Italy, Edmundo, a customer service receptionist at their hotel, helped them acquire and refine some more essential language. As Geoff recalls, "We found our daily interactions with him so delightful. We developed a special fondness for him, and we maximised our opportunities to get sight-seeing advice while talking with him and learning more Italian – always hilarious!"

Beautiful Venice moved Geoff to capture poetic images, rich and romantic like watercolour paintings, as well as images of intriguing Venetian characters in unique moments of time. Both Geoff and Toni remember this part of their trip very fondly too.

The next trip to San Francisco in 2006 was a lot of fun for the whole group of water polo husbands and wives. Geoff recalls, "As with the Italian competitions, the team was able to win the odd game, but no medals. The San Francisco travel experience was very different to the Italian trip. It was interesting and educational, but we were surprised to see so much poverty and so many drug-affected street people, which took the shine off some explorations. However, we were able to enjoy a huge number of exciting, fascinating art galleries, particularly in Union Square, as well as a lot of public musical performances, including some excellent busking. As for the water polo events, I loved the challenge and excitement of team competition."

Chapter Thirty Three

Life at home

By 2009, Geoff had had a photographic studio in Hay Street, Subiaco in Perth for about eleven years. Robyn, his sister, worked full-time for him there, expertly helping run the studio. Toni was working as a naturopath. The children had all reached adulthood. The two girls, Emma and Jasmine, had moved to Melbourne for new, independent adventures, and the boys, Brendan and Ashley, were living in Perth. At this time, Geoff and Toni were living at 24 Reeve Street, Swanbourne, and I was briefly sharing the house with them while I was between houses.

With the move to Swanbourne, Toni and Geoff decided to buy two Devon Rex cats, after their previous one died. Toni has an allergy to some cats, but loves them, like Geoff. The Devon Rex breed is quite small and 'non-allergy' with soft, extremely short fur and a furless, pink tummy. Because of this relatively furless state, it needs to stay warm, so likes to be cuddled all the time – even in summer. For extra interest, the breed even looks like E.T.! The new sister-brother kittens had to be flown from Victoria, which we soon understood had caused them to develop serious PTSD. They were very skittish, highly reactive to noise and fast movement, and they remained that way. The brother named Yoko, dominated his sister, Omo – yes, that is how they named them – but when Yoko died, Omo became slightly calmer.

Geoff's photo of Omo and Yoko (L to R!)
Swanbourne 2009

At the same time, after investing in a Thermomix (a cooking/blending device) and finding it a boon in the kitchen for its efficiency, as well as its nutritional and economic benefits, Toni trained as a Thermomix consultant. She believed the consultancy could increase her earning capacity, and married well with her naturopathic knowledge and cooking skills. Geoff was supportive because he could appreciate the benefits it would provide. And … they both just love gadgets of all kinds. However, the work was not financially rewarding enough to continue.

Chapter Thirty Four

Fitness, friends, and more ...

As usual, Geoff was keeping his routine, swimming with friends, early before work and on the weekends. These swims were frequently in pools, either at Christ Church Grammar School, Davies Road public pool in Claremont, or more often at The Superdrome – since renamed Challenge and then HBF Stadium. Often, they were in the ocean, swimming the return trip between Cottesloe and North Cottesloe beaches, with the requisite coffees enjoyed afterwards.

Dedicated team of lunch-time swimmers, UWA pool
Late 1990s

Geoff (front-far left) with Kirby Swim adult squad,
Claremont Superdrome, 2002

Some of these swimming friends have been fellow cyclists. Most of them have intense professional occupations, which likely results in them needing some equally intense stress release in the form of sport … nothing like worthy pain, chased with endorphins into a state of relaxation! The challenges involved in sport are important for their personalities, and sharing the activities they love bonds their friendships. As they weave their way through Geoff's continuing story, several of these friends are referred to, frequently by first name only.

Geoff (front left) with the Lycra brigade at Old Papa's, Fremantle, 1990s

Trouble brewing

One evening, late in May 2009, after a game of water polo, Geoff returned home and told Toni: "There was an incident at the pool today when one of the guys had a bit of a turn, so Robert took his pulse, which was 220, and it appeared he had an arrhythmia."

Later, he told Toni that 'one of the guys' was really him. He explains, "I was trying to introduce the concept, trying to soften the blow."

The next day he had various heart tests with cardiologist swimming friend, Mark Ireland, and at that point nothing showed up, so he was given the all clear. He and Toni had a party three days later, and Geoff didn't drink any alcohol, which Toni thought out of the ordinary.

Chapter Thirty Five

An unforgettable event

The next day, 1st June 2009 – Foundation Day (now Western Australia Day) and also Brendan's birthday – Geoff was training with swimming and water polo friends at Challenge Stadium, doing 300 metre sets.

"I suddenly felt unwell, attempted to rest my head on the lane rope, but seeing myself going down – then I blacked out. The others saw me sinking and quickly dragged me out at the end of the pool. It was forty-five minutes of trauma for Robert and the others who helped resuscitate me with CPR. They tried to get the one defibrillator, which was in a locked cupboard in the office at the front of the pool, quite a distance away. They brought it down, only to find they had the wrong bits and had to go back. In addition, the oxygen tank was almost empty.

"A few people called an ambulance which had to come from Dianella instead of just around the corner at 'Charlie's', for some unknown reason. The ambulance took a long time to get to me because they weren't sure which entrance to come to. There were gates at the side very near to my location, but they had to come to the front of Challenge. It took the ambos, with their big defibrillator, to get my heart going during the ride to the hospital. The worst aspect of the whole thing was that they later gave me my speedos back cut in half!"

While all of this was happening, Toni was having a coffee with the wife of one of Geoff's team-mates, Diana Vitasovic, at the Dome café in Cottesloe. Some of the swimmers were expected to join them there, but after some time when they didn't turn up, Diana took Toni home, both somewhat perplexed. A little later at home, Toni answered the door to see Diane again and her husband Brian looking very sombre. Diane said, 'Toni, you'd better get your bag and come in the car with us. Geoff's in hospital.'

Knowing about Geoff's incident the previous week, Toni felt shaky with shock, and didn't want to ask for more detail, afraid they would say he was dead, or dying. When they arrived at the hospital, in the emergency waiting area, a group of the swimming friends were standing there, some still in their speedos, all looking worried. Robert Larbalestier supported Toni and led her into the emergency room to see Geoff. Apparently, one or two of the nurses present were 'admiringly gobsmacked' to see Robert arrive in his speedos in Charlie's Emergency Department.

Toni remembers, "Geoff was lying in a bed with tubes up his nose and medical attendants all around him. One of the doctors asked me what he had had for breakfast, and when I answered 'black coffee' they were relieved because he had black stomach contents, which can indicate internal bleeding. Later on, he was put into an induced coma under an ice-blanket for twenty-four hours, because ice slows down a degenerative process called 'reperfusion'. Then it was a 24-hour wait until it was time to wake him up, to see if he had impairment to his brain and faculties. Waiting was painful, and I felt like I was in my own suspended state of animation."

Fortunately, although I was shocked and worried myself, I was able to support Toni at home and regularly drive us to the hospital. This was necessary, as Toni was not wholly in her own body or mind for some time.

Mates star in heart-stopping pool drama

Robert Larbalestier kept his mate Geoff Fisher alive for 45 minutes when his heart stopped in the pool at Challenge Stadium.

The 61-year-old Subiaco photographer had swum 1.2km in training with members of the City Beach Polo Bears when his friends saw he was in trouble.

Robert, a heart and lung transplant surgeon, was among those who caught him, hauled him out of the water and started to resuscitate him with chest compressions.

"He did not have a pulse," Robert said.

Also on hand was Anne Brinkworth, medical emergency team co-ordinator at Sir Charles Gairdner Hospital, and other trained professionals.

"If you are going to have a cardiac arrest, Geoff did it with all the right people around," she said.

Geoff and Robert joked about the rescue this week when Robert visited his friend in Sir Charles Gairdner Hospital.

Three of Geoff's ribs were broken during the CPR.

"We've got a few doctors in the group and I asked Robert if we had a lawyer so I could sue for my broken ribs," he said.

"But seriously, I owe everything to Robert and everyone else who helped.

"How do you thank someone for saving your life? The words come out but they don't sound adequate."

The heart surgeon and the photographer have been friends for about eight years since Robert commissioned Geoff to take photographs of his family and then joined the water polo team.

Robert said three others helped him keep Geoff's heart going.

"You have to do it hard and fast," he said. "If you are really doing it properly you cannot do it very long at all."

Steve Redbond, a Cottesloe surf lifesaver, and another doctor each took five minutes stints with Robert, pumping Geoff's chest.

"All resuscitations are confronting and you have to focus on what you are doing," Robert said.

The friends kept going with the manual resuscitation while staff tracked down the stadium's heart defibrillator.

Centre manager Rob Verboon, another friend of Geoff's, said there had been a delay of about seven minutes because the machine was at the opposite end of the complex.

He said stadium staff used a two-way radio to call for the heart machine but a new member of staff could not find it in the reception area at the front of the stadium.

• Please turn to page 70

Geoff Fisher, right, has heartfelt thanks for Robert Larbalestier who helped save his life.

Pool drama

• From page 1

A staff member ran the 200m from the pool at the back of the complex to get it.

Mr Verboon said staff followed emergency procedures and called an ambulance and evacuated swimmers from four other pools.

The procedure for emergencies was for a staff member to meet the ambulance at the main entrance.

"I think there have been some second and third calls for the ambulance by other people who may have suggested it enter via McGillivray Road," he said.

He said staff called him at home nearby and when he arrived at the stadium he found it was his friend being put into the ambulance.

"He is very close to all of us at the stadium. He has done a lot of work for us as well as using the facilities," Mr Verboon said.

"There were some human stresses involved."

Since the incident a second defibrillator costing about $4000 had been bought and was now stored at the back of the complex, he said.

Geoff is now looking forward to a jog on the beach, and says staff have kept his business, Fisher Photography, ticking over as usual.

His sister Robyn, who helps him run the business in Hay Street, Subiaco, said Geoff was in an induced coma on a refrigerated bed for 24 hours.

Nurses in the intensive care unit told her Geoff's temperature kept rising.

"I said he is so rebellious it was typical of him," she said.

Robyn said her brother was irrepressible.

"Although Geoff is in hospital, he has managed to call us most days and still has his business hat on."

Geoff said he played water polo, swam four days a week, cycled and went to the gym in-between.

He has swum to Rottnest and played waterpolo most of his life.

He said he had had a cold and felt odd while swimming the week before.

Minutes before he collapsed he had made a swimming sprint to catch a mate's flippers at Challenge Stadium.

With kind permission from Post Newspapers Vol. 36 No. 25, June 27, 2009.

Intensive Care Unit

Geoff remembers, "As I started 'coming-to' in the ICU as they brought me out of the coma, I could hear voices."

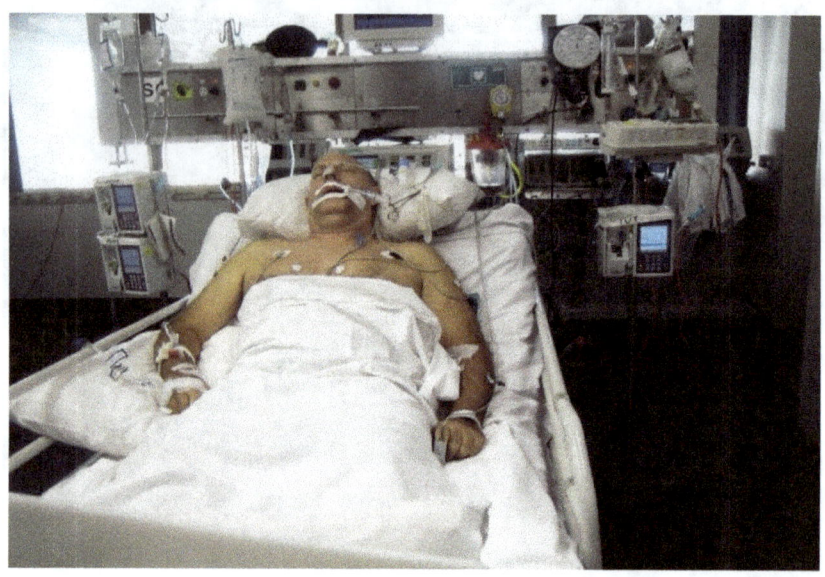

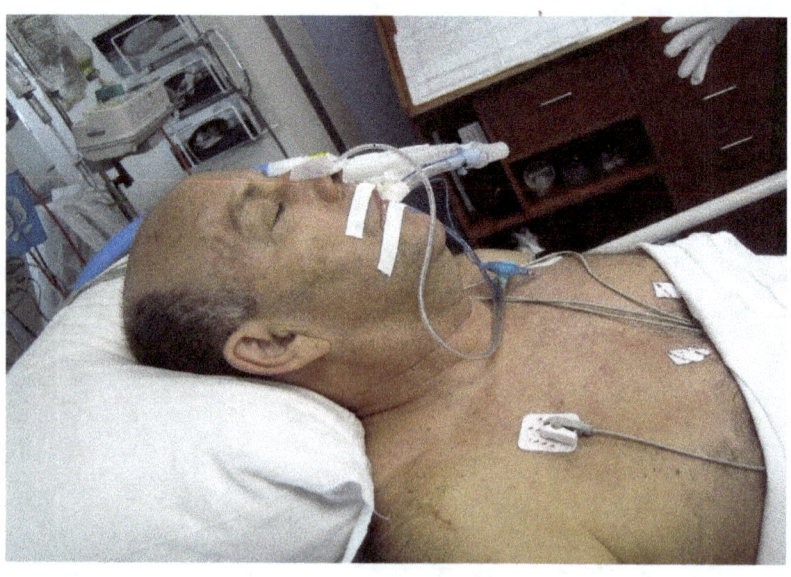

Next, the doctors asked him if he knew why he was in hospital. We watched as he responded by making breaststroke movements using both arms, followed by a downward plunging motion, showing that he knew exactly what had happened. The relief felt by us all was palpable.

He remembers, "I had all these tubes up my nose and down my throat, so I used sign language. I must have known Toni was there. When she jumped in front of me and startled me, saying 'Hello, darling!', I just managed to ask her who she was – that was a joke – I did that and smiled, so she was even more relieved. They all knew I had good brain function then. Robyn and you Eve were there too."

A moment after our brief reunion, one of the attending doctors came to check Geoff's right-left brain function by asking him to raise both of his arms as high as he could, which he was able to do straight away. The medicos in the room expressed amazement and were thrilled. In our more recent interview, Geoff joked that, "If I had known that they were going to do that test, I would have put one arm up, and then changed them around!"

With Geoff's agreement, Toni informed Brendan, Ashley and Jasmine as soon as they could manage. However, they were in a quandary about whether to tell Emma, who was travelling with her family in the USA, in New York at that time. They knew she was enjoying her time there and didn't relish giving her the upsetting news, but they soon decided they had to tell her too. They had to leave a message initially, as Emma was in a completely different time zone. Geoff vividly remembers, "Emma called back from New York and there were long pauses, because I was unable to say anything. It was very difficult, very emotional for us both. She was obviously anxious, especially being so far away and I was choked with emotion."

Brendan and Ashley were able to visit Geoff in the hospital and, although shocked, were able to deal with it better by having seen him. Jasmine was in close communication and regularly kept up to date throughout. She offered to fly to Perth immediately, but was told not to come then. Her travel would have caused great expense and work disruption for her. In addition, Geoff was intensively involved in his treatment, procedures and physiotherapy, not knowing how each minute, hour, day or night would eventuate. At that time, he was preoccupied with his pain, his medical issues and his own emotional state.

Having survived the initial event, followed by Emergency Department treatment and then ICU, Toni and everyone else were greatly relieved, but still very concerned, not knowing how things would progress. Geoff was kept in ICU for a few days and a couple of weeks in the cardiac ward. He had a very unstable heart, and painful broken ribs from the extended, yet expert CPR he had received from his highly capable medical swimming friends, notably Robert and other qualified practitioners. Broken ribs are often necessary collateral damage in such cases.

Chapter Thirty Six

Cardiac Unit

Jig-saw pieces

After a range of investigative tests, it was decided that Geoff needed a defibrillator-pacemaker, which was inserted under the skin of his upper left chest, wired to the heart.

Geoff explains, "The pacemaker makes the heart muscle contract and creates a rhythmical pulse with electrical energy. Its function is to pace the heart and increase the pulse when appropriate. The defibrillator's function is to correct erratic rhythms. It doesn't work all the time, like the pacemaker, but is on constant stand-by. I had cardio-myopathy leading to my heart arrest, but hadn't been aware of the condition. My heart failure was a gradual process, developing over at least ten years.

"In a way, it snuck up on me. It took something big to realize I was in trouble. In the World Masters Water Polo Championships in 2008, I remember that at half-time in a game, I was in the middle of the pool, and I lay on my back and I felt really, really stressed heart-wise, and I thought to myself that if I was ever going to have a heart attack, this would be the time. But, I realized that from years earlier, my heart had been going downhill and I just thought I couldn't get enough air all the time. I didn't really suspect that I had cardiomyopathy, because I'd never heard of it anyway. Now

I'm much more tuned-in to people who complain of chest pain but then ignore it.

"A little while before I had the cardiac arrest, I remember riding to water polo on my racing bike and going up the hill through Perry Lakes, in Floreat. As I got to the top, I was having a problem. I had a rhythm change in my heart, which must have been an atrial fibrillation (A.F.). It gave me a fright. I was aware that I was by myself, and that if I carked it there and then, nobody would know. I rode on to water polo and played in a subdued manner. I couldn't keep up with everybody else at swimming either, and I didn't know why. I later saw photos of myself at the end of the pool having made an effort, and being red in the face. I had been sucking in air the whole time and felt exhausted."

"When I went to Italy in 2004, I had other problems. My muscles were so stiff, I could hardly move my arms or throw the ball, and I thought later that it must have been because my cortisol levels were too high, causing inflammation. But I was also aware, as Toni has reminded me so often, that sugar is also pro-inflammatory! I had the same problem when playing games in our local competitions. When someone was swimming over the top of me, kicking and pushing me backwards, which is part of the game, I was in agony, because my body was aching so much.

Toni adds, "There is something called the 'sports-person paradox'. This refers to a person who takes fitness to the extreme, who can become over-fit with an addiction to adrenalin and endorphins, while ignoring stress and ill-health signals."

A few nights before the heart arrest, Geoff had photographed a wedding. He was ignoring his depleted condition. By the time he finished, he was happy with the photos, but exhausted. This was simply one of the extra straws that broke the camel's back.

While in hospital, doctors discussed the possibility that he had had a viral infection at some point which had impacted his heart.

Geoff reflected, "In 1972, when I was in Alice Springs, I became ill with a fever, headaches, muscle pain and shakes. Initially, the medicos thought I may have contracted viral meningitis which would require a lumbar puncture, but for some reason they decided not to proceed. I was glad about that. And I wasn't sure about that proposed diagnosis, because I had also had a health episode when I was exposed to chlorine gas through a mini explosion at the Alice Springs public swimming pool around that time. The incident was written up in the paper. I was admitted to hospital to monitor my blood toxicity and breathing.

"As well as that, in 1996 or 1997, when we lived in Forrest Street, Cottesloe, I had another serious episode with the same symptoms, and water polo friend, Dr Glen Koski, dropped in to check on me. He said he would palpate my spleen, to which I replied, "I haven't got one!"

The spleen produces red blood cells which carry oxygen for the body. It also has a crucial role in immunity. Many in the medical field were amazed that Geoff had been able to participate in so many endurance sports with such a handicap, although an x-ray initially suggested that Geoff had a bit of vestigial spleen tissue. However, a later x-ray revealed that he had no remaining spleen tissue. Regardless, concerning his illness, his malaria-like condition simply appeared to be '...one of those mysterious viral infections'.

Geoff had yet another resurgence in 2008, when we all shared a home together in Floreat. For a couple of days, he had felt generally unwell, until he suddenly went into rigors. Toni had to put him into a hot bath to warm him up, and the rigors slowly subsided, although he continued to have severe headaches with cold shakes, and fell into tears at times. He recovered little by little over several days. It was evident that some kind of virus had been dormant in his system, and we assumed it was Ross River virus, or the like, because of the symptoms. Nevertheless, it remained an assumption – general blood tests provided no answers and doctors did not pursue that line of enquiry.

Chapter Thirty Seven

Legs

While in the Cardiac Unit, it became obvious that Geoff's legs didn't work, and that the issue was more than just weakness caused through lack of exercise. This was a very dramatic blow and Geoff did a lot of crying, not understanding why he couldn't control them. Initially it was thought he could have had a blood clot in his spine, causing damage to the nerves in his legs. However, later this was reviewed. The diagnosis was that Geoff experienced a lack of oxygen to those extremities during his heart event at the pool. In emergencies, the body automatically withdraws circulation from extremities to maintain function of the more vital organs, such as the brain and heart.

Doctors, nurses, family and friends were highly supportive and attentive. Some very kind nurses often sat on his bed at night, having heart-to-hearts to let Geoff express himself, and to keep him company. I gave him frequent kinesiology and reflexology treatments throughout his hospitalisations, and an expert masseur visited him a few times.

Long days and nights

Geoff had a constant stream of family and friends visiting, many of them taking care to check with Toni first, or with Geoff directly. Being such a gregarious person, the company of others was usually his best medicine, although there were times when he felt he couldn't be 'available' to visitors, dealing with his own depressed feelings and considerable pain.

Toni remembers, "One day Geoff told me not to visit him, and I was so devastated with my own raw feelings and anxiety, that I rushed over to our friends, Gary and Claire Ward, to just cry and feel their support. In better days, I realised it was too needy of me, too selfish in the circumstances."

Geoff recalls how he felt at that time. "Every night I asked myself, 'How do I get through the whole night?' There was one occasion when the same friends, Gary and Claire, came to visit me late in the evening, which was lovely. I was in constant nerve pain in my legs, and I didn't know how I was going to get through the night, so when they left, it was like being abandoned. A feeling of panic came over me, and I cracked up. I was in tears, and that was a very dark time. There was more happening during the day, but at night it was just pain and anxiety and whatever else I couldn't help thinking about."

On 25th June, one of his good friends, journalist and news reporter Gary Adshead, provided some welcome distraction when he interviewed Geoff about his dramatic experience for The West Australian. Geoff recalls, "It happened to also be the day that Michael Jackson died, but the article about me beat the news about Jackson by a few hours, because when the paper was printed, Jackson hadn't died yet. My interview was published, first with a large photo on page three and the larger report following on page nine. That was one of those 'Yes!' moments. Gary and I were very amused."

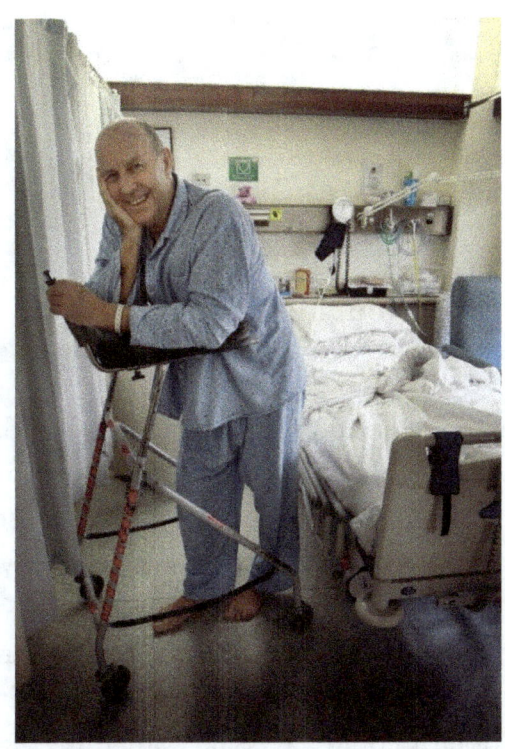

Copyright permission: The West Australian (WESTPIX TWA-0126225)

News
thewest.com.au

Medics pool talents to save fellow swimmer

GARY ADSHEAD

Award-winning Perth photographer Geoff Fisher died three weeks ago and lived to tell the tale.

After he had a sudden cardiac arrest during a routine swim at Challenge Stadium on Foundation Day, it took about 15 minutes for staff to find the venue's lifesaving defibrillator and 25 minutes for an ambulance to arrive.

While the 61-year-old now faces the challenge of getting back the use of his legs, he was lucky enough to have a heart surgeon swimming metres away and specialist medical emergency co-ordinator Anna Brinkworth had just arrived for her morning exercise.

With another doctor, who was in the pool, and a long-time triathlete — who was wrecked for up to 30 minutes to save Mr Fisher's life.

"We'd started swimming away from and were about half way through when I felt a bit dizzy and could feel something coming on," he said.

He collapsed to the bottom of the pool before being grabbed by swimming colleagues who thought he was playing a trick on them.

One was cardio-thoracic surgeon Rob Larbalestier, who worked tirelessly with the others to keep his friend alive using expert CPR.

"I've got three broken ribs to prove it," Mr Fisher said.

"I have been told the defibrillator wouldn't be found but I was unconscious and don't know enough of the facts. I just know I am a very lucky man."

Challenge Stadium chief Rob Yorston, also a friend of Mr Fisher's, told The West Australian yesterday he was disappointed with the delay in getting the quickest access to the stadium. Mr Yorston got the staff down to appeal information provided by a range of physically fit people other than lifesavers.

"A code blue was correctly called by the staff, an ambulance ordered for a priority one and the defibrillator was called for," he said. "It was called for immediately but we had a staff member who wasn't sure where it was, which meant our aquatic staff had to come up and get it. I agree that the time delay was unacceptable and we have bought a second unit to place nearest the outside 50-mtr pool.

The defibrillator was then used to shock Mr Fisher's heart but his life continued to hang in the balance.

An ambulance, which was coming from Subiaco because closer crews were already busy, had trouble finding the quickest access to the stadium. Mr Verbrugge got shut down to sequel information, provided by a range of physically fit people other than lifesavers.

"I think it's fair to say that with the doctors there and Anna Brinkworth working with her qualifications, Geoff was in touch with God," Mr Yorston said.

Mr Fisher spent about 24 hours in an induced coma with doctors concerned he may have suffered brain damage.

"Paul would have been a common outcome for what had happened to him," friend Peri Malcolm said. "In the end, he has come out of it with his mind functioning well, but with this conviction for his legs. A blood clot to the base of his spine cut off oxygen to his legs and he's unable to walk at this stage. It's a question of what nerve damage has been done, but Geoff's not about to throw the towel. His determination is more than is impressed."

Mr Brinkworth said Mr Fisher's story is miraculous because she believed if not for the people around him at the time for weekday's later made it. "This is proof that learning CPR and having defibrillators easily accessible can save lives," she said. It was not acceptable to have to wait that long for the defibrillator. The earlier you defibrillate the more chance you have to revert the brain on electrically able rhythm. I know in his case he was still lucid and go when he went to the ambulance."

The Subiaco-based portrait and landscape photographer said he had begun the rehabilitation process and pleased to return to his studio soon.

"The business is still open and staff and friends are working so hard to keep it all going," he said.

Copyright permission: The West Australian newspaper (WESTPIX WAN0039662)

Chapter Thirty Eight

Neurological Ward

Geoff was transferred to the Neurology Ward, still within Sir Charles Gairdner Hospital. His neurologist in attendance, Dr Blacker, when checking Geoff and discussing his condition, said he thought Geoff would probably never walk again.

"My friend and colleague, Ric Syme was visiting me at the time, and was quite devastated about the situation. He thought the doctor could have said something like, 'Well you could have a lot of problems, but if you give it your best shot, you might be able to walk in some capacity.' That is what I wanted to hear, not just negatives. The physiotherapists also said to me, 'You'll probably have to use walking sticks or a walking frame for the rest of your life.' That could have been true in some cases, as from their point of view I had no strength in my legs, but I was very determined."

Clearly, none of them knew who they were dealing with! The prospect of not walking at all was shocking and unacceptable to this dedicated sportsman and active, social being. Although deeply disturbed by the possibility, he would not surrender his sense of humour.

"One day I attempted to trick Dr Blacker, who came around with a group of quite serious medical students to check me in the neuro ward. He asked one of the students to check my signs, and gave him the knee hammer. He hit my right knee at the reflex point, at which point I made my left pop up. Although the students were being tested, they all cracked up, which lightened the mood."

Geoff had some control of his quadriceps, so could manage such a corny practical joke, even though his body was weak. Soon he was given a high-tabled walking frame with castors, called a pedestal walker, to support him to walk as upright as possible. It was inspiring to see him using it, pushing it forward with the weight and force of his upper body, enabling his legs to follow in a walking motion.

Typically, whatever distance he was told to practise, he would double it, regardless of any discomfort. Getting out of bed and onto the walking frame was a difficult process in itself. In addition, because his bladder nerves were weakened then, he had to be catheterized, unpleasant at best, but he soon had to learn to do it himself, daily. It was expected that he would have to continue this at home. This procedure caused some anxiety. He didn't know if he would ever get normal bladder function back. He had a lot to deal with. Toni told him they would do whatever might be necessary going into the future, that they would adjust and carry on together, no matter what. She emphasised that he was still the same person, still the same man she loved, no matter what lay ahead.

The neurology ward was a depressing environment for Geoff's recovery. A lot of patients there had had brain injuries and strokes. Many could not walk or talk. Geoff explains, "One man there had encephalitis and he couldn't speak or function normally. He had worked for CALM and had contracted it, probably from a mosquito. His family made a recording of a cat purring for him to listen to, to comfort him."

Nevertheless, Geoff soon had his room-mates laughing most days.

A Post community newspaper reporter visited Geoff in the ward to interview him about his heart arrest at the pool and his experience beyond. Apart from family visits and interviews, he was often visited by work colleagues, close and extended friends, water-polo and swimming mates, old riding friends, caring clients and neighbours. Sometimes these visits allowed shared entertainment for the other patients, brightening the mood in the whole room, while at other times caused consternation for hospital staff who had to medically attend to Geoff, and hoped for more order.

With delight, Geoff recalls, "On one occasion, a close friend, Shane McGurk, took in a collection of masks and dress up gear from his school. He played at interviewing me while we both wore the gear, creating hilarious characterizations in the process. It was very funny and a great distraction. Shane videoed our funny acts for me to watch again later. The video has provided more laughs over time and is a great memory of our friendship."

Another swimming friend, Paul Malcolm, thought it would be welcome relief for Geoff to have an outing, to go for a coffee by the ocean he loves, in Cottesloe. Geoff wanted to go, so with hospital permission and Toni's help, the plan was set to take him in his wheelchair to their familiar seaside café, Barchetta, in Cottesloe. Having negotiated Geoff into his wheelchair in the hospital, they then had to get him out and into Paul's car, but they discovered how extremely difficult this was, because Geoff could not stand up on his own.

As Toni clearly recalls, "He just started falling down like a bag of stones! We eventually got him into the car and took him to Barchetta, but then we had to get him out of the car and into his chair, when he was falling down again. He was still recovering from his broken ribs and lacked exercise, so his usual upper body strength was not available to him. Nevertheless, we managed to get him inside to a table, at which point he fell into tears that he couldn't stop. I saw a woman near us looking at him, and I stared back with daring in my eyes: 'Don't look at him or else!' I was trying to block the woman's line of sight. I felt very protective, which can be my tendency, although Geoff tells me it's not necessary."

All three – Paul, Toni and Geoff himself – realised that, although it was a very caring endeavour, it was still too ambitious. At that early stage, Geoff simply didn't have enough strength.

While in the Neurology Ward, Geoff fully acknowledged that his legs didn't work, with zero movement in his legs. This disturbed him deeply. He recalls, "If my leg fell off the bed, which it did, I'd have to reach over and grab it and bring it back by my pyjama legs. When I got to the neuro ward, one of the things I did, was to turn over onto my stomach. This was very difficult – I had to get onto my hands and knees to see if I could support myself, as if to crawl. I was very wobbly. I could easily fall off the bed. I thought to myself, 'Well, that's interesting. How am I going to manage this?'"

Geoff was in Sir Charles Gairdner Hospital for two months during which he recovered from his broken ribs and received a pacemaker and defibrillator. He had to start coming to terms with his acquired walking disability, his constantly painful legs, and uncertain loss of some bladder function. At the same time, he was unable to work, of course.

Chapter Thirty Nine

Shenton Park Rehabilitation Hospital

Onto the next destination, Shenton Park Rehab, which was an annexe of Royal Perth Hospital. Geoff was given a wheelchair and transferred there from 'Charlie's'. He was put in a room with other incapacitated patients, mostly brain injured. The hospital was generally referred to as 'Selby' because it was on Selby Street in the suburb of Shenton Park. The majority of its patients had had motorbike accidents. It had a depressed, sad reputation. It smelled of old cabbage. It had bland green walls with restricted spaces. It felt closed-in everywhere.

"My room was windowless, and I think it was originally a store room. Some of the other patients couldn't speak, or couldn't walk. One man in my section had had part of his skull removed, which apparently was put in a fridge and had 'gone off', so he then had a section of metal skull put in. He had been there for eighteen months, wearing a helmet."

On his first night at Selby, Geoff said they took his wheelchair out of the room, parking it in the hallway, supposedly so that it would not be in the way in his confined space. Stuck in his narrow bed that night, he was confronted with a sudden feeling of utter powerlessness.

"I had my first-ever panic attack. I felt I couldn't protect anyone in the event of an emergency, such as a fire. After dinner-time, when the chair was taken away, I had no means of escape or transport and I couldn't get away, and that's when I had a meltdown. I was devastated. I think I had PTSD. But I had my laptop with me, so later I was able to get lost in the movie Dark Knight, which alleviated some of my anxiety."

Geoff remembers feeling very stressed, initially, when going to the physiotherapy gym there. "For my treatment, I had to try to pedal on a stationary bike, and at first I pedalled backwards instead of forward – my legs refused to work normally. Then I switched to weights on pulleys. For this, my feet were attached with Velcro straps to a resistance device with small weights to produce muscle tension, to help the adductors in my inner thighs, but they had to take the weights off. Then they had to take off the thing that holds the weights. Then there was just string. I was struggling to pull the string across, as required, which I thought was funny."

"During one of these times, my wedding album supplier, Gary Jorgensen, came to visit and thought he'd help, so he held the string. While at his mercy, he asked me if I'd paid his bill that month! – and we had a good laugh together. But another time, I was trying my best to do a kilometre or two on the bike, but it was so difficult that I just fell into tears of frustration. I was struggling.

"Each day I went to the gym, I would try to go further and further. Eventually, I managed three kilometres with no resistance, a good measure of my recovery. Then I did floor exercises, similar to Pilates. If the physios asked me to do ten, I would do twenty, which felt really rewarding. At one stage later, at the gym, I went to the toilet in my wheelchair and I could stand up to have a wee for the first time, which felt amazing, and I started yelling to myself in celebration!"

While in his little, cramped room with three other male patients, Geoff sought ways to interact with them and support them. He told us, "One man had had a stroke. The only words he could utter as they craned him out of his bed in the middle of the night to go to the toilet, was 'Fuck!' When I passed by him in the mornings, he would usually have some numbers and letters in front of him. His therapy was to say the letters, so I would say them first and he would copy me. He could say some of the letters correctly, but others were mixed up. It was very difficult for him.

"The nurses came and went all night. They were short-staffed. Often the nurses argued in the corridor about who was or wasn't pulling their weight. They talked and made so much noise at the station next to my room. They weren't very happy and many were struggling to do the work. And the kitchen smells of old over-cooked cabbage wafted up the hallway to our room.

"Some days were 'low activity' days, which seemed unfair to the patients, to all of us in need of exercise. Exercise and general activities are so important for dealing with grief, depression and boredom.

"Eventually, one of the orderlies helped me get to the therapy pool, a small heated pool where I started doing laps. The female physio heard that I was doing fifty laps instead of ten, and being concerned, went to check on me. At first, I said I'd only done twenty, but then admitted I was doing fifty or more. The problem was that most patients couldn't do much at all with their brain injuries, and in some cases, it was not appropriate. But for me, it was so much easier to roll my arms over and it was such a short pool. I wasn't stressing my heart, so it felt comfortable. I'd just do as much as I could do. I'd been longing to get into the pool. Before, they would say

'Oh, yeah, well, we'll let you do that soon', but it was never soon enough!"

Often there were three or four days with nothing for the patients to do. Geoff often went to the pool, requiring him to get onto a hydraulic platform that lowered patients into the pool. Geoff eventually took himself there and lowered himself in, so that he could maintain his lap swimming exercise, as well as to relieve tension and boredom. The staff got cross with him for his independent 'can do' attitude and behaviour. He acknowledged they were worried about his heart, but he believed it was exactly what he needed.

Rehab at Selby 2009

Selby finally released Geoff with a critical letter which said that, 'He kept doing sixty laps in the pool when he was supposed to do ten'. He explained, "They stated that whatever happened to me as a result, was up to me, and was not their fault ... that because I would not co-operate, they could not be held responsible. The letter did not refer to the little picnics on the lawn outside the hospital, or the few beers smuggled in, but it is likely this was part of their reasoning too. It was akin to being expelled from school.

"One night I was visited by Robyn, Helen Adshead and Izabela from Mirage photo laboratory. They suddenly appeared in my confined room and proceeded to pull my pathetic curtain around to create a zone of pretend privacy (The Cone of Silence – not!), and out came stubbies of beer and chocolates. Everyone felt very naughty! As for the picnics, it was reported that I'd been naughty again, because Helen and Gary Adshead with their two lovely young boys, Harrison and Ben, with Robyn, Toni and Eve, created a little picnic-party out on the lawn.

"I remember being pushed around in my wheelchair by Helen and Gary's young boys." (Harrison and Ben always called Geoff 'More Cake' for some reason!) "We had fun and it was some light relief. The staff wasn't very happy, but I didn't care. I just thought they were too conservative, too old school."

On another occasion, Ric Syme and partner Marianne, together with Robyn and Toni, took some beers and nibbles to create 'an outing' on the Selby lawn for friendly support and welcome distraction.

Ric Syme, Geoff, Robyn and Marianne at 'naughty picnic'
Selby Rehab Hospital 2009 – (Toni taking photo)

"I didn't like being in a wheelchair and I didn't want to get used to it. The temptation was to learn to move the chair like wheelchair sports-people do – tilting the chair up, turning, and going backwards at speed, doing tricks in it, which is a real compensation for physical freedom. I refused because I knew I wasn't going to be doing it for much longer."

Overall, Selby staff found him a bit too rebellious for their 'system'. The family wondered how often someone was expelled from rehab.

Chapter Forty

Let there be light

Geoff was an inpatient at Selby in 2009 from the end of June until August. Early in August, he was given 'day release', when he could go home for a meal and to cuddle the cats, usually during the weekend. Day release was impactful. In marked contrast to the hospital environment, their home was welcoming, colourful and aesthetically pleasing, with soft sunlight filtering through French windows which opened out onto a cloistered courtyard.

Geoff was anxious to get home, but had mobility issues there in his wheelchair. It was an emotional experience every time. He didn't want to go back to Selby, but he soon progressed to 'full weekend release'.

Toni recalls, "During one release visit, I went out briefly to the shop, and when I returned, I found Geoff had wheeled himself almost into the front courtyard, at the doorway, facing north. He was in the nude, basking in the sunshine. The light was so perfect, I took a photo. Then, sometime later, while I was consulting a naturopathic client in my home office, that nude picture suddenly appeared on my screen as a screen saver. I panicked. My client was awkwardly trying to pretend that she didn't see it, and I couldn't turn it off quickly enough!"

Fortunately, the house in Swanbourne had two large

lounge rooms, one of them at the rear of the ground floor which was slightly 'sunken', having two steps down from the main level. Close by on the main level was a quite spacious toilet room with wash basin. Negotiating those steps with the wheelchair was not possible, so Geoff pulled himself up backward and over the steps on his bottom, using his arm strength to get there. He used walls and available objects to brace himself to move up and around as he needed. Soon Robyn's son, Quito, a carpenter, brought his welcome skills and made a wooden ramp to cover the steps for Geoff's wheelchair. (Geoff commented, "I could see aspects of my younger self in Quito.")

Toni had hired an electric bed for Geoff, set up in the back lounge room. These temporary additions made his release visits possible, and relatively comfortable, but the main bedrooms and bathroom were upstairs. There were fifteen steps to ascend and descend, making the upper-level destinations out of reach for a while.

"When I was home one weekend, on Grand Final day, Robert came to visit and I tried to get up from the lounge room sofa, to stand up and walk two steps, but I crashed to the floor, and had the most excruciating pain in my left leg that I could ever remember. I just had to lie there – in a cold sweat – and wait for the pain to subside. Eventually, I climbed back into my wheelchair, but as for my leg strength – there was none. I thought I could stand up and hold my weight, but couldn't do it safely."

Finally, Geoff was released from Selby as an inpatient for good, with physio out-patient visits regularly scheduled during the week. Toni or Paul would take him there, and home again. If they weren't sitting by the pool or in the gym with him, they found ways to entertain themselves in the interim – they drank a lot of coffee and read several books then.

As Geoff incrementally regained more upper body strength, he managed to get up the stairs to the bedroom and bathroom, but he could not use his legs or feet to push himself up. "I went up the stairs backwards using my arms and hands, pushing myself up on my bottom.

The 'fifteen steps challenge' – Swanbourne 2009

When I got to the top of those fifteen steps, I'd roll over and crawl to the bedroom and drag myself up onto my tummy, roll over and then lift my bottom onto the bed. It was quite an ordeal each time and I was sweating profusely by the end. Next, Toni would bring the wheelchair upstairs to the bedroom so I could wheel around to the bathroom, which had a high-sided bathtub with shower overhead. Then I'd get into the bath from my wheelchair."

Geoff needed a support board put across the bathtub to rest against, to stop him slipping down, as he couldn't stabilize himself with his legs. Although Toni helped him, getting in and out of the bath was a significant challenge and took a lot of strategic energy. Geoff still had substantial body weight to manage as a tall, well-built man who had, most fortunately, kept his upper body relatively strong with his lifelong swimming and continued efforts to exercise.

Often, when Geoff pushed himself to complete a physical task, such as getting up the stairs and onto the bed, he was left depleted, crying. Many things triggered tears and this worried him, but he didn't stop trying to improve. He didn't give up. He always wanted to maintain his positive attitude, his default position in life, although some of his medical friends were concerned that he wasn't really dealing with his emotional issues. He wanted to enjoy being with his friends, sharing his good humour and camaraderie, but at times he was depressed, anxious, and crying a great deal.

Throughout everything, Geoff took heart from all of his achievements, great or small. During a visit from Brendan and Ashley, Geoff asked them to try getting up the flight of stairs in the same way he had to. Although they were both youthfully fit and strong, they struggled to make it to the top - which entertained them all.

Ashley and Brendan, Swanbourne

Yet, Geoff remembers there was a bigger dream.

"At one stage Robert said he could see me walking up those stairs and I said, 'Yeah, I agree', but inside, mentally, I was thinking, 'I don't think I'll ever be able to do that! At the time, even though I was determined, it just seemed like an impossibility. I thought it would be like climbing Mount Everest. It was not that I thought I wouldn't have a go at it. I thought, 'Yeah, well, that would be great, but …' A few months later, I realised that dream, drawing on a lot of arm strength."

Chapter Forty One

Studio concerns

It was very hard for him to accept being in this mental and emotional state. Part of his depression was due to feeling his loss of role in the studio and being worried about the business. He was deeply grateful for the generous support he was given at the studio by Robyn and others. Robyn was employed to professionally manage clients' appointments, payments, photograph selection sessions, put photos in folders, file negatives and a range of other essential duties. Their sister-brother bond worked well on many levels. Amongst inevitable frustrations in the workplace, they also shared a constant stream of jokes and laughter which drew in others around them, and occasionally evolved into a party atmosphere.

Another employee, Leanne Hay, did the regular bookkeeping, which helped to keep the vital 'money in and money out' numbers clear. David Coote, Geoff's accountant, continued to take care of the more serious figures. Many photo shoots were very kindly and expertly done for Geoff by his friend and colleague, Ric Syme. Other photographers included Henrik Tived, who worked at the studio, as well as Angie Coote, Kate Drennan and Janet Craig, who he contracted to do several shoots for him. Geoff trusted them all for their professional skill and competence, and couldn't thank them enough.

This studio support meant he could focus more on his health and progress, while knowing that the business was being cared for. He was in regular communication with the studio, usually more than once a day, wanting to be actively involved in decision-making and fully in touch with operational activities. But he really loved doing his photographic and studio work. He missed his lively interactions with staff and clients and his creative photo shoots. The studio was being kept afloat, but he didn't know what his own physical outcome would be, or when he would be there working full-time again. He was also the main breadwinner and he had always been proud of that.

Chapter Forty Two

Being a survivor

Geoff's outpatient experience continued for two more months, while he regularly used the physiotherapy facilities there. Although he was happy to be living at home again, he fell into depression. He felt very guilty for leaving his roommates behind. After having spent such close time with them, sharing experiences with them, supporting and empathising with them, he then felt he had abandoned them to their fate.

Seeing the awful effect this had on him, I thought at the time that it was akin to 'survivor guilt' so often felt by soldiers who return from war, or by people surviving other devastating situations. He had already experienced similar guilt when he left the Neurological Ward at Charlies. Geoff became emotionally fragile and started having panic attacks in the early hours. He didn't know what to do about them.

Our sister, Leith, kindly visited during this period, and stayed with them at Swanbourne. As much as Geoff normally enjoyed seeing her and spending time with her, he could not climb out of his depressive and anxious state of mind at that time. It was not how he wanted to be. He was sorry that he could not be socially available to her, as they had previously shared entertaining, positive times together.

This was a very difficult time for Geoff. Nevertheless, throughout his troubles, he remained focused on his goals.

Every physical negotiation, every stretching or bending movement requiring balance, and with considerable pain, remained an important challenge in his rehabilitation. When he dropped something, whether in the hospital or at home, he insisted on finding his own way to retrieve it. He would not let others pick it up for him, or simplify the task.

He comments, "I always kept my conscious mantra: 'The more I walk, the more I can walk.' I could live with that." In fact, Geoff applied the essence of his mantra to all his abilities.

Geoff's friends, David Coote and Paul Malcolm, often drove Geoff quite a long way for treatment with a Professor of Chiropractic to help him with his recovery. Toni said, "Although Geoff often claimed he was unsure of his progress from this treatment, I often witnessed significant improvements in leg movement over the time he had these sessions. But I know it can be hard to gauge one's own seeming 'slight' improvements."

While physical needs predominated, it was vital to care for his creative needs. To keep Geoff stimulated and engaged with his photography, Toni often took him to scenic places such as King's Park and Cottesloe Beach, where she pushed him around in his wheelchair so that he could enjoy taking photographs. And in a never-give-up way, he took on some family portrait shoots from the wheelchair.

Toni recalls, "Sometimes he would clamber out of his chair and get down onto the ground to negotiate better angles for his clients. The best image was essential to him and he didn't let pride get in his way. He didn't worry about what any observers thought. But I was apprehensive about him taking photos at the beach, on the sand, where he eventually used his elbow crutches with the risk of falling over. But I never tried to deter him. When he did fall over, some people appeared to be embarrassed for him, but he was not embarrassed himself."

Geoff's own photographic therapy – capturing abstract view, North Cottesloe

This has always been Geoff's way. He may feel vulnerable, and he may witness the objective degree of difficulty facing him, but being always determined, he just keeps working toward positive outcomes. However, Toni adds, "In contrast, at times, there is a surprising exception to this: a perceived or actual critical comment by someone directed at Geoff may evoke a very stinging rebuke!"

One day, when Geoff was at home and feeling down, his friend and swimming coach, Bill Kirby, picked him up for an early morning training session. He recalls, "When Bill arrived, I wheeled myself out to his car. This required me to stand up and hold on to the roof rack while he packed the chair in the back. Bill was opening the back up and to our collective surprise, noticed the wheelchair had taken off down Reeve Street. Bill ran frantically down the hill to catch the 'getaway chair'. Luckily, he managed to grab it before any damage was done. It was all quite exciting! We got a good laugh out of our little drama."

With time and effort, Geoff made significant progress and became stronger. He graduated from the wheelchair to elbow crutches, then to using two walking sticks. This part of the journey took about six months. During this period, Toni's personal life was very much on hold as she transported Geoff to rehab appointments and to the studio for work. So, when Geoff was given permission to drive again, able to express more independence, his morale improved markedly. His general heart health proved stable at that point, so he was given a practical test by a G.P friend, to assess his driving capability. "I was asked to put my feet on the doctor's feet. Then I had to press firmly on 'the accelerator pedal' and 'the brake pedal' to demonstrate my leg muscle capability. Then I had to put my hands up to show I was moving 'the steering wheel', and make 'bbrrr, bbrrr' sounds as I was 'driving'. We both finally fell about laughing at this absurd scene! In fact, while driving in the beginning, my right foot occasionally drifted off the brake pedal on left hand bends, so I had to lift it back into position with my hand."

Geoff's ability to drive and tangibly engage in work improved his morale, restoring much of his enjoyment and enthusiasm, although there were still some challenges in work demands. It had been enormously stressful for Geoff to be away from his studio, his staff and the creative work he loves.

He was eager to get back to a swimming routine, his other source of spiritual nurture, fitness and challenge.

Driving meant that Geoff had more freedom and was feeling more competent, but then Toni felt quite bereft. She asked herself, "What should I do now?" For so long, her days had been devoted to Geoff's needs and routines. She realized she had to adjust her full-time role as carer. She had to refocus to some extent, to create some new, meaningful activity in her spare time.

Toni continued to help at the studio sometimes, in different ways, as she had done throughout Geoff's hospitalisations. Robyn's work role there was vital as she kept the t-s crossed and the i-s dotted, helped manage many administrative details and client needs – and sometimes her brother! – while still sharing plenty of humour and positivity. Friends and colleagues also visited them at the studio, contributing to its familiar jovial atmosphere.

Both Geoff and Toni felt deeply grateful to his sister Robyn and photographer colleagues, particularly Ric Syme, Henrik Tived, Ian Cheok and Angie Coote for giving so much. Geoff had maintained constant communication with them throughout his hospitalisations and recovery. As far as practicable, he had engaged with staff to make necessary decisions, but when his physical presence and contact were not possible, they had to manage based on how they knew Geoff wanted his business to operate. He could not have sustained the business without their loyalty and dedication. There was definitely a lot of love in that support.

In impressive time, however, Geoff progressed his mobility, even though he could not hold himself upright for long without stable supports.

Robyn recalls, "The toilet was outside the main studio building and there were a couple of different floor levels involved, so when he had to go to the toilet, it was fun and games all round … He used his wheelchair to get to the step at the back door. Then he held onto the wall, grabbed a bar at the rafters supporting the tin roof, and swung out like a monkey. I always felt nervous while waiting for his safe return. I knew that he couldn't stay upright if he tripped and needed to step backward or sideways suddenly – or simply lost his balance. Sometimes he tripped." The rest of the negotiation is unclear!

Apart from the studio and his photographic work, Geoff maintained activity to the best of his ability in the pool and the ocean, constantly supported by his swimming friends.

At Kirby Swim with Shane McGurk

At the beach, he initially crossed the sand with his walking sticks, then negotiated his way slowly into the water where he could again be his oft' used swimmer nickname 'Fish'. Exiting the waves at shore often required a little more help.

Geoff's heroes - Robert Larbalestier and Annie Brinkworth, helping him out of the water, Cottesloe 2011. They were primary in saving Geoff at Challenge Stadium.

Geoff was taking drugs for constant nerve pain in his legs, which played havoc with his mind and emotions for the first couple of years. When he was released from Selby as an inpatient, he was taking prescribed Pregabalin for nerve pain, and Oxycontin – both highly addictive prescribed drugs. He was determined to get off them as soon as possible, knowing what he would have to endure in the process. When he stopped taking them completely, he experienced profuse sweating with shakes, while rolling around in pain on the bed. He concluded, "Trying to get off them must be like trying to get off heroine."

It took about three days for his worst symptoms to abate, but he still had terrible pain in his legs, frequently feeling extremely cold. Toni bought him a thick Kathmandu beanie, fleecy jacket and mountaineering socks, as well as an electric heated blanket for his legs. He had to use these while sitting in front of a heater, in spite of the warm weather outside.

With several factors at play on his mind and body, Robyn and others working at the studio had to deal with his bossy and difficult behaviour at times – not a completely new experience, but intensified at this time. Yet, whatever the stresses at the studio, the 'crew' always found ways to have fun. Robyn relates one of their traditions, which was to have 'Junk Food Fridays', or alternatively named, 'Fat Food Fridays'! This meant that at 12:00, for lunch, all the staff would head off to get sausage rolls or pies and tomato sauce – Geoff would get as much tomato sauce as possible (as he still does). They enjoyed their secret junk food together with lots of good laughs. Of course, there was plenty of other illicit food (usually sweet) consumed during the week.

However, Toni would often turn up at the studio with something fresh and healthy, like sushi rolls, asking 'Would you like some lunch?' to which Geoff would say, 'Oh, yes, I'm really hungry', but he usually fell about laughing with the others. Toni eventually gave up trying to make a difference there on Fridays.

The Hay Street studio in Subiaco was a very welcoming, attractive space that people enjoyed entering, much like Geoff's previous studios which were also attractive buildings, with aesthetically pleasing décor. Many people – family, friends, colleagues and clients – have happy memories of being there. Geoff also held successful exhibitions of Anne's work to encourage her to keep painting in her late 80s, all creating colourful, happy memories.

However, the studio was now carrying extra debt, and finances were extremely tight, requiring serious juggling. Geoff has always been a hard worker, inspired and successful, and good at earning money. Yet, saving money hasn't always been his strong suit, for which a more laissez-faire, living-in-the-moment attitude has prevailed. Toni shares some of his carefree nature, and money seems to be mercurial for them both. However, Toni comments, "Geoff is highly organised with his photography shoots, as with his wardrobe and drawers, where everything is prepared and arranged 'just so' and monitored perfectly."

Like Geoff, at times, Toni attends to minute, demanding details requiring supreme dedication and determination, particularly when required for a creative project – in strong contrast to some of their other 'caution to the wind' forms of expression.

Following Geoff's illness and hospitalisations, the future of the Hay Street studio was uncertain. Everybody involved continued to be hopeful while continuing to do their very best, in spite of the stresses. Geoff had to use his wheelchair until November of 2009.

Geoff at work in Hay St studio

Still so many jobs to do!

Geoff with his underwater photo of Robert
Copyright permission: The West Australian newspaper (WESTPIX WAN0039661)

In 2010, when he was able to walk with sticks and was getting more mobile, his daughter Emma and her partner Ben Flavel decided to get married, in Melbourne. The family in Perth were invited. This meant Geoff had to fly, then walk the vast distance through Tullamarine Airport. Even Toni and I found the trudging distance demanding after the flight, but Geoff still refused to ride on an airport service buggy, and did not want us to wait for him along the way. He stubbornly and slowly made his way, with only minor rests to catch his breath. It took a lot out of him. Fortunately, we were able to taxi to a hotel and rest until the next day.

The wedding took place at a high position in a lovely park in Carlton. Geoff had to escort his daughter down the red carpet laid on the grass using his two purple walking sticks, taking great care not to trip. Even that walk was a huge effort for him, but he wouldn't have had it any other way. He was so happy to be able to be there. He was able to get rides to the formal restaurant reception nearby where he spoke as father of the bride, and then to the concluding tavern celebration. Toni recalled that while walking over one street crossing, he tripped and fell. True to type, he did not dwell on it, but managed independently to get to his feet again and carry on.

Father of the bride, Emma with bridesmaids Jasmine & Dan
Carlton, Victoria, 2010

Shocks

Back home in Perth, although Geoff was improving in strength and mobility, he started to experience some strong shocks from his defibrillator, which he found very uncomfortable and upsetting. Of course, the defibrillator was doing its job properly, however disturbing.

At one time, when Jasmine was able to visit and stay with Geoff and Toni at Swanbourne, she witnessed Geoff having an arrhythmic episode. Jasmine was cooking in the kitchen while Geoff was leaning over the servery bench, advising her on some camera skills, mentoring her for her own freelance photography business. As they were chatting, Geoff suddenly let go of the bench and slid down onto one knee before collapsing completely to the floor. Jasmine was mortified and rushed around to help him.

Geoff explains, "I had a moment's dream as I came to consciousness with Jasmine's face in my face, urgently calling 'Dad! Dad! Should I call an ambulance?' and I said 'No, don't bother. Toni will be home in a minute. She can drive me." Toni returned shortly afterwards and drove Geoff at her best speed on the over-familiar route to Charlie's Emergency.

Similarly, Geoff remembers further occasions of having to race to Emergency with arrhythmic episodes, in which Toni was driving her trusty little silver Echo. "I felt like crap and she wasn't driving fast enough, and I said, 'You can put your foot on it, love. Let it rip!'" Toni felt conflicted, driving as fast as she could while staying within the varying speed limits. Every time, they rapidly rolled the windows down to pull in as much fresh air as possible.

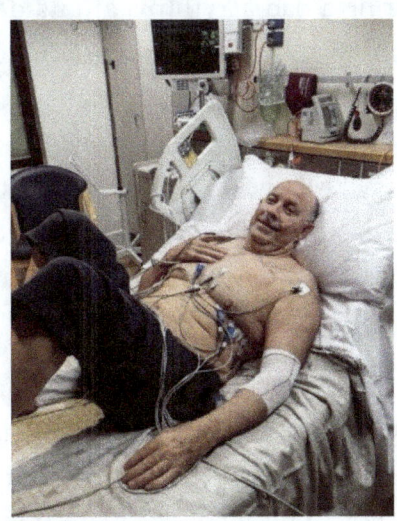

Geoff wired up.
Pacemaker and defibrillator still in left upper chest.

Sometimes they had to go to Charlie's in Nedlands, sometimes to the Mount Hospital in the city, while at other times to Hollywood Private Hospital in Nedlands, and much later to Fiona Stanley Hospital in Murdoch.

At times when Geoff felt whoozy, often as if about to faint, Toni would accusingly ask him if he'd drunk too much coffee, as he tended to do, or she would quickly give him something suitable to eat to help balance his blood sugar level. Unfortunately, such 'relevant-in-the-moment' interim remedies progressively lost their relevance as Geoff's arrythmias increased in frequency and intensity. He had both atrial and ventricular fibrillations, but mostly atrial.

In addition, his defibrillator had to be adjusted at certain times. To adjust it, a strong magnet was used for a procedure called 'interrogating the device' in which the defibrillator is disabled to allow an unaided assessment of heart rhythm. Geoff depended on the defibrillator to keep his heart working, so to disable it was frightening.

One time, during a bad arrythmia after a defibrillator reset, he recalls: "I would look at the ceiling wondering if it would be the last thing I'd see. Then the nurses would say, 'Try and relax and think of something nice', but I was thinking about dying. Then I'd say, 'Oh, yes, I'll think about that lovely nurse who was on duty last night!' and we'd all have a laugh."

Serial shocks

One night, at home, when Geoff was downstairs watching TV and Toni was upstairs, Geoff had a major arrhythmic event. His defibrillator triggered, giving him some powerful shocks in succession. These shocks were traumatising and he felt like he was dying after the first few shocks. He yelled out for Toni who was in bed upstairs, and she then flew down in the nude, pleading, "What can I do? What can I do?" to which Geoff urgently replied, "It's going to go off again!"

Geoff's anxiety became Toni's panic. She asked if she should call an ambulance, but at first Geoff said no, until the third shock.

"Then, as it went off again, I urged her, 'Call the ambulance, unlock the front door, get some clothes on!" Toni immediately called 000, then tried to find out if he had been doing something that contributed to the event, like watching a disturbing movie. He admitted that he had been watching Django Unchained!, saying, "The defib went off with a bang during the closing scenes when a lot of people were about to be massacred, and at the same time our cat was throwing up in front of the television!"

It is also important to understand that to deal with Geoff's growing anxiety, he had to take medication which played havoc with his other emotions too.

As it happened, Geoff and Toni learned later that Robyn's daughter-in-law, Marita, was working at the emergency phone-line response centre at that time. She received the ambulance request which was identified as 'critical' and Geoff was taken by ambulance to Charlie's nearby. When Geoff was finally stabilised there, he was still able to amuse himself by revisiting the image of Toni flying downstairs in the nude!

"But the ambulance trips weren't good either. It was like riding in the back of a truck. They're sprung fairly hard, so rather uncomfortable. Besides that, having my defibrillator go off five times in the ambulance, after ten times at home, was really shocking! But I simply had to deal with it as it happened. We can't go back to 'What if this? What if that?' We just have to survive. And lots of people go through that every day, all over the world. It's survival mode."

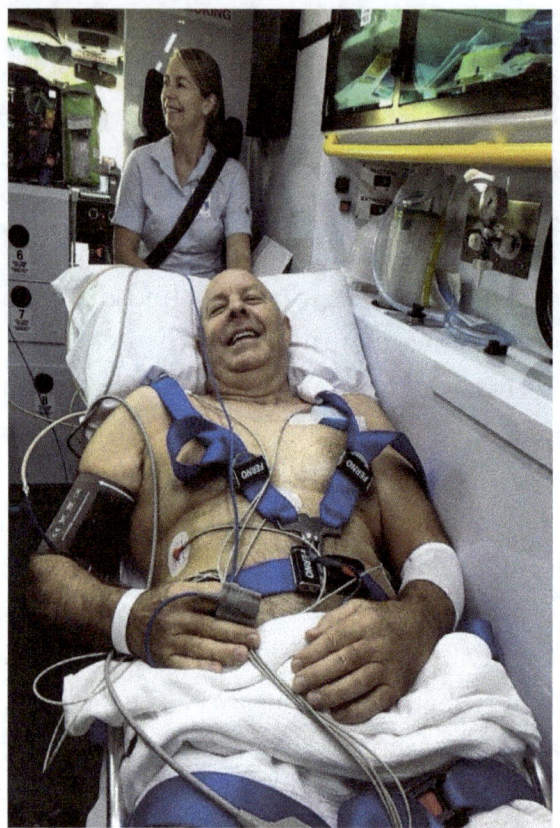

Yet another ambulance trip between hospitals for scans!

Chapter Forty Three

Ablations

Geoff was soon transferred to Hollywood Hospital which led to him having another medical intervention. Clearly his pacemaker and defibrillator were keeping him alive, but the arrhythmias were so frequent, that another procedure to improve his heart function was considered. He was advised that an 'ablation' was recommended. Ablations involve cauterising the surface of damaged heart muscle to remove scar tissue that interferes with normal rhythms. They are performed under anaesthetic.

Geoff was weak and anxious when he went to Hollywood. "I was mentally prepared for the ablation to be helpful, and when I was wheeled into theatre, I was amazed at all the lights and high-tech equipment – very impressive. But when I was wheeled back to the ward, waking up, I had so many feelings. I was a bit numb, and my whole upper body felt traumatised. Trying to breathe normally was pretty hard, and stressful."

Geoff was administered the required drugs and constantly monitored by medical staff, who also commented on his equally constant business and social phone calls, conducted in spite of his challenged physical condition. At every opportunity, he typically had humorous interactions with hospital staff and other patients he met, engaging on a first name basis.

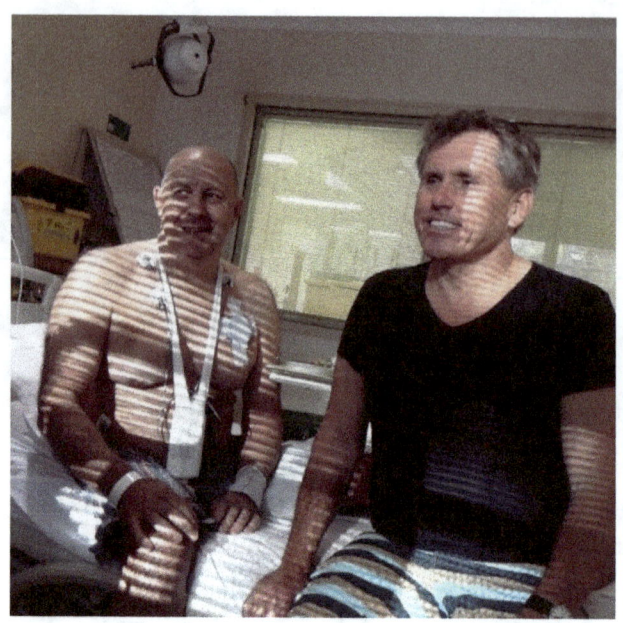
After ablation, friend Shane McGurk visits, Hollywood Hospital

Second ablation

"When my heart activity settled down, overall, I was released from Hollywood, but my defibrillator would shock me every now and again. I still felt uncomfortably weird, light-headed, or dizzy. The shocks were always unsettling, but I had to get on."

By this time his heart was swollen, oversized, unstable and with further loss of function. Geoff was feeling his subsequent lack of oxygen. His breathing was more laboured. His continual arrythmias led to him having a second ablation at Hollywood. It was much the same as the first. As Geoff clearly recalls, "Waking up from those operations was difficult and painful."

The ablations took a high toll on Geoff, particularly the second one. When Toni and I visited him in the hospital afterward, we met him in the foyer where he was trying to walk a little, but I thought he looked deathly grey. He could barely walk and seemed to have lost his spirit. I was deeply worried. Of course, there were inner strengths and determination at play. After a few days, he started to recover his strength and personality.

"I accepted that I had to have many medical tests. I know that when I was in the cardiac ward at Hollywood – and I was there quite often – the nurses made comments about all the phone calls I used to make. They were work and social calls. I remember that when I was on the gurney, waiting to have my old heart scanned, I was making business calls in the holding area, organising portrait sessions and things like that … Never say die!"

However, with his release from hospital, in his tenuous physical condition, Geoff had to deal with growing anxiety for which he was prescribed Diazepam, a form of Valium. He used to keep some in his pocket because he started to get anxious about going out in public, something so very contrary to his basic personality. He was anxious that he could have an arrhythmic episode in a place where he didn't have the normal supports to deal with one. He constantly tried to manage what amounted to post-traumatic stress disorder (PTSD), compounded since his cardiac arrest and all of its consequences. One day, he and Toni went to see a movie with close friends, Margot and Kim Roberts, but he had to go outside for a while to drink some water, take a few breaths, as he calmed himself and waited for this to pass. This was a new and disconcerting event for him.

Also, for the first time in his life, Geoff experienced episodes of anxiety in the ocean and in the swimming pool, his favourite environment. While swimming, Geoff started imagining scenarios in which his heart would stop, asking himself, 'What will happen to me? Who will find me? How long will it take them to get me out of the water? How long will it take for an ambulance to get me to hospital? Will I survive?'

After his second ablation, Geoff's heart still went into uncontrolled rhythms for a couple of days. This caused loss of appetite, nausea and emotional and physical distress. Later, as an out-patient, Hollywood gave him a course of group counselling sessions to better manage his panic attacks. They proved helpful.

Geoff in difficult times with Robert and Gary helping raise spirits
Swanbourne 2011

About five years after his initial defibrillator had been inserted at Charlie's, the doctors decided to give him a new upgraded one with a third lead to increase effectiveness. However, due to scar tissue resulting from the ablations, the procedure was very difficult and the third lead could not be inserted at the time. A little later, at the Mount Hospital,

Robert had to insert it through the shoulder with a drainage tube inserted into Geoff's lower left side. Later removal of the tube was quite painful, but he was pleased to find the upgrade was a good improvement on the old model.

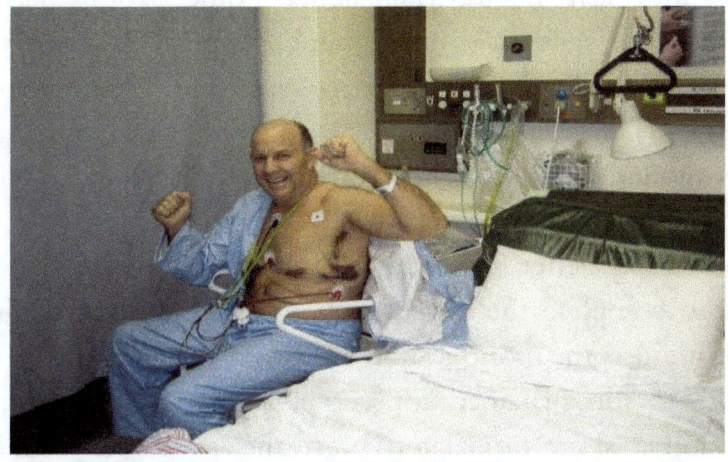

Recovering from insertion of new defibrillator at the Mount Hospital.

King's Park

Geoff continued working at the Hay Street studio. On one occasion, he was engaged by clients to do a photo shoot for their large family at King's Park, and Toni also went to assist. As it happened, the group included a couple who were a surgeon and nurse.

Before leaving home in Swanbourne, Geoff said that he had started to get uncomfortable feelings, including sweating and feeling like he could fall over. When Toni, more than once, questioned the wisdom of going out, he replied, "I'll be alright." However, during the shoot, the surgeon noticed Geoff's excessive sweating, so approached him to take his pulse, promptly saying, 'You've got to get to emergency straight away!' Consequently, Geoff was not able to finish the session. The couple quickly took Geoff in their car to Charlie's Emergency Department and Toni followed them.

Although this incident was another example of Geoff's perseverance and of 'believing in the best', he was actually going into heart failure when he left home. From Charlie's, he was then sent on to the Mount Hospital's Cardiac Unit where he was given an intravenous infusion of Amioderone overnight to stabilise him.

Amioderone has a positive effect on the thyroid, which in turn has a positive effect on heart function. Geoff felt considerably better for some time after this infusion. He was able to complete the family's photo session successfully at their home some months later. However, the infusion's effect could not be sustained for very long, so he had another infusion a short time later. Nevertheless, sadly, his heart continued to lose basic function.

Leaving the Hay St studio

In 2013, Geoff had to let the Hay Street studio go. He had to work as best he could from home in Reeve Street, Swanbourne. He continued to rally himself to do all the photographic work he could manage with Toni's help or Robyn's, but he also arranged for a few photographers he knew well, and trusted, to do some assignments for him. He created a home office upstairs and Robyn worked for him there every Friday, assisting with the business for about three months. She found other employment for the rest of the working week. Leanne also did the bookkeeping there when needed.

Soon, Geoff could hardly walk out to the front of the house, could barely stand up. Just walking a couple of metres from the front door left him breathless and weak. Every activity was a huge effort. His whole life was becoming severely compromised. Nevertheless, he still sought work and found ways to do photo shoots with Toni's assistance. His skills and creative vision remained intact, but he became less able to walk without gasping for air, even around the house. Panic attacks were frequent, especially at night when he could not breathe properly as low heart function meant he could not clear fluid from his lungs, even when using a CPAP machine, raised pillows, and other strategies. Hospital emergency visits prevailed when breathing difficulties and anxiety became too much to bear. This was also very traumatic for Toni, who was in a constant state of hyper-vigilance.

Chapter Forty Four

Fiona Stanley Hospital

Eventually, Robert Larbalestier, Mark Ireland and Gary Ward said Geoff could be better managed by the specialized heart team at Fiona Stanley Hospital. It is a dedicated Cardiac Failure Unit with a specialized cardiac gym in which both outpatients and inpatients can exercise, while being closely monitored and guided. However, when Toni first saw that the unit was called a 'cardiac failure' unit, she was shocked and upset and said, "They shouldn't call it a 'failure' unit!"

Geoff was able to talk to other patients using the gym, patients who were hoping or waiting for a heart transplant, or had already received one. He was constantly dreaming of the possibility of having a heart transplant himself. In the meantime, Geoff and Toni decided to move much closer to Fiona Stanley, as the regular long drives from Swanbourne were taking their toll. In addition, they could not get an ambulance to take Geoff to Fiona Stanley while they lived in Swanbourne.

The move

They knew they had to move to a single storey home, leaving those fifteen stairs for others to climb. They found a comfortable, one-level unit in Attadale, just ten to fifteen minutes from the hospital which greatly relieved the time-

and-distance driving pressure on both of them. However, the big move from Swanbourne was very stressful in itself. Geoff's physical efforts during the move were naturally very limited, but family and friends pitched in with generous support, sorting, cleaning, packing and transporting everything. Toni and Geoff were sad to leave the Swanbourne house, but were glad to say goodbye to the stairs and the inconvenient lawn.

Celebrating Geoff's 70th birthday, before leaving Swanbourne, August 2017

Once settled in Attadale, their sense of relief was palpable, as they felt so much more secure being close to Fiona Stanley, knowing they could quickly drive there and get an ambulance easily.

Even before the move, they had spent a lot of time waiting in Fiona Stanley Emergency, always impressed by how the staff and Cardiac team treated Geoff, by how 'switched on' they were. They had found all the doctors and nurses to be intelligent, well-informed and compassionate. They felt very safe in their hands, together with Robert's amazing team.

The Cardiac specialist gym was very supportive for Geoff and he attended at least three times a week, although sometimes he didn't even have the strength to open its heavy entrance door. At the gym, there were usually some people exercising with their new hearts. Geoff often talked with gym staff to learn as much as possible about fitness outcomes for transplant recipients and occasionally managed to talk with new recipients. He was determined to maintain as much fitness as possible to be eligible for a new heart, not knowing if he'd survive long enough to receive one.

Sleeping at night was fraught. Even when Geoff could fall asleep, he was usually restless. At one point during his 'waiting' experience, Emma's family made a welcome short visit to Perth to stay with Geoff and Toni. But one night during their visit, Geoff's breathing became very laboured. When Toni asked, "Are you alright?" he insisted he was. Not believing him, she asked, "Should we go to the hospital?"

He was sitting on the side of the bed then, but getting annoyed with her questions. So, desperate to get a night's sleep herself, in spite of her worry, Toni resorted to taking a sleeping pill – for the first time – and went fast asleep. However, in the middle of the night, Geoff developed a higher level of anxiety about his breathing problem and finally felt the need to go to the hospital. He tried to wake Toni up, but she didn't respond.

In the morning, Toni woke up and couldn't find Geoff. She looked everywhere inside and outside the house, but he was nowhere to be found. She was concerned and perplexed. Then she received a text saying, 'It's a lovely morning over here at Fiona Stanley!'

Geoff had not wanted to disturb Emma and the family in the night, so he had decided to call an Uber. Dressed in his shortie pyjamas, he had walked down the driveway in the dark to the street and had taken himself to Fiona Stanley's Emergency Department. He stayed in the hospital for another night and was settled with a medication adjustment. Toni still felt very guilty. When she told Robyn about it all, Robyn replied, "What? You didn't really take a whole pill, did you?" – but Toni had already realized her error by then.

Shortly after this, when I visited them, I felt upset to see Geoff barely able to walk a metre or two to the front door, struggling to breathe properly. His energy and spirit were seriously depleted. His weak condition with difficult breathing events continued.

During this period, Geoff had a 'reversal' procedure at Fiona Stanley, in which his heart was shocked back to a normal rhythm while he was anaesthetised. On this occasion, he learned that his 'ejection fraction' (E.F.), was as low as 10%. Normal E.F. is around 55%. E.F. measures how strongly blood is pumped from the heart. The reversal helped him for a limited time.

Everyone was increasingly worried about him. Toni was 'living on the edge' emotionally as she watched Geoff struggle and decline each day and night.

Chapter Forty Five

On the list

Toni remembers, "During one of Geoff's regular clinical appointments at Fiona Stanley, the medical staff suggested that they may be able to put him on the heart transplant list. This gave me a huge fright! Geoff was at the extreme end of potential candidates, being seventy years old, but he felt very hopeful and was more than willing to go through a range of extremely thorough and protracted tests to determine his viability.

"He had to 'pass all the tests', which included his brain, teeth, eyes, vascular system, bones, all of his organs, skin and nails. He had to visit the dentist to get a complete dental health report and to have any fillings or other matters resolved. He had to have brain tests too. For some of these, he had to go into machines that required his defibrillator and pacemaker to be turned off. This made him nervous, as he depended on them to keep him alive. Nevertheless, he came through all of the tests with flying colours. Apart from his heart condition, his overall health and fitness were excellent. His test results were then discussed at a heart team meeting in which Robert, according to policy protocol, was not allowed to have input."

The cardiac board decided to put Geoff on the candidate list, with surgeon Chris Merry assigned to do the transplant, but they were concerned about whether a suitable heart could be found to match his large stature and body type. In addition, there were other essential biochemical details, such as antibodies, required for a match. Much of this is more complex than most people can understand. Receiving a suitable heart, or any organ, can be like finding the Holy Grail. There is a lot of dedicated work performed to test and assess suitability of both the recipient and the donor organ to make any transplant a realistic possibility.

While Geoff felt very excited by this positive development, and hopeful, Toni felt very worried. In floods of tears, she sought the support of friends.

First call

At one point after Geoff was put on the candidate list, he was informed that the cardiac team had a possible donor heart for him, so they needed him to prepare. Then Toni hurried to the hospital with him to have his chest shaved, but half way through the night they said, 'No, sorry, it's not a good enough match.' They had to go home, not knowing if Geoff's fate would be like some patients who expire while waiting for a suitable heart. As Toni said, "All the ducks had to line up for it to be a possibility."

Geoff was very disappointed, but he simply focused with positivity on the next one! He knew there was no promise of a matching donor heart and that his health was seriously declining, his breathlessness increasing by the day, but he maintained a hopeful outlook.

First waxing

In hospital for tests Geoff remembers, "… As a nurse shaved my arm and chest for some new tests, I suggested that she just keep going and take the whole lot off and she happily obliged … It seemed sensible because every time they came and stuck things on me, they'd have to rip them off. So painful. The movie '40-Year-Old-Virgin' came to mind. My empathy for the actor Steve Carell grew immensely. Unfortunately, when I went back to hospital, the hairs had grown again, so it didn't make much difference at all – it was just as bad the next time!"

Chapter Forty Six

And there was more

Since 2009, Toni had cared for Geoff and had felt she could not leave him alone for extended periods, but in recent years her left knee had become more painful and increasingly unreliable. She thought it was destined for surgery, but could not foresee an opening for this. Only when she could barely walk unaided, did she feel forced to seek a specialist's opinion, and possible surgery in spite of Geoff's very weak condition. Her orthopaedic specialist recommended an immediate total knee replacement, noting the very poor condition of her knee. She was left with no reasonable choice.

After Toni's operation and nine days in Hollywood Hospital, Geoff collected her himself. He had to negotiate her into the car from a wheelchair, then out again at home, while caring for her swollen, highly sensitive leg. He did not have much extra strength of his own to support her, but he managed. It was just forty-eight hours before their next very big event.

Some phone calls are better than others

Geoff recalls, "Toni had just got home from hospital with her completely new knee, and could hardly move. She was in pain and drugged up to the eye-balls! So, I went off driving around to get a walking frame and other things to help her manage, when I received a phone call from a nurse at Fiona Stanley. She said, 'Are you by yourself?' and I said, 'Yes'. Then she asked me if I was driving and if so, to pull over, which I did. Then she said, *'We have a heart for you!'*

"That was very exciting – the special news I had been waiting for since October. It was 9th February 2018. She said, 'Can you be in hospital in an hour?' and I said, 'Too right, I can – I'll be there!' So, I drove home and sat down with you Eve, and Toni. You two were getting anxious that I wasn't ready to go, that I wasn't moving quickly enough … but underneath I was very excited that I was setting off for this new adventure."

Toni and I thought he may have been exercising his 'oppositional self' then because we were urging him to hurry up – to no avail. Geoff always resists others' inclinations to panic. It seems we really were the only nervous ones. As Geoff simply comments, "I packed a minimal amount of things because I didn't think I'd need anything for ages, just a toothbrush and a shaver, my phone and phone charger."

I drove us all to Fiona Stanley in my little blue Toyota Yaris, Geoff in the front passenger seat with his lightly-packed overnight bag, acting as navigator, with Toni arranged horizontally, placed ever-so carefully along the length of the back seat with her crutches and handbag. It was the first time I had driven to Fiona Stanley. Geoff advised me to stay within the speed limit, having 'plenty of time' – and honouring Robyn's pleas not to speed – as we took the shortest route to the hospital.

After getting Toni out of the car, I found a wheelchair, parked the car and joined them both. With all the difficulty involved, Geoff joked, "I should have just got an Uber!"

Next, we all proceeded, stopping long enough to take a

photo of 'the happy couple' on this most memorable day.

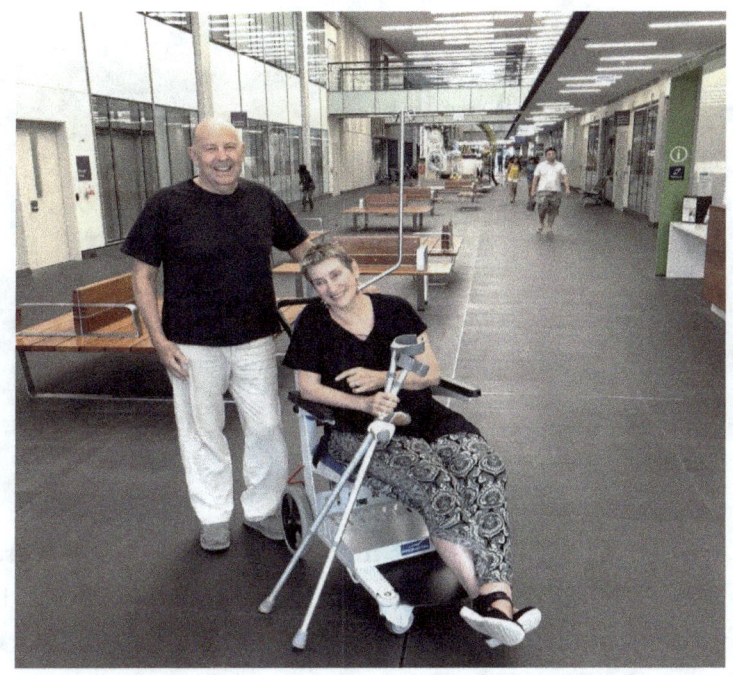

Arriving at Fiona Stanley Hospital on that very big day!

I had quite a challenge negotiating the awkward wheelchair with Toni's painful leg jutting out. Not surprisingly, she was extremely nervous about her leg hitting walls. The confined lifts were the most difficult to manoeuvre in, but we survived to tell the tale later with a sense of humour.

We arrived safely in Geoff's room. We put Toni in a stable chair and Geoff climbed happily onto his bed, mobile in hand.

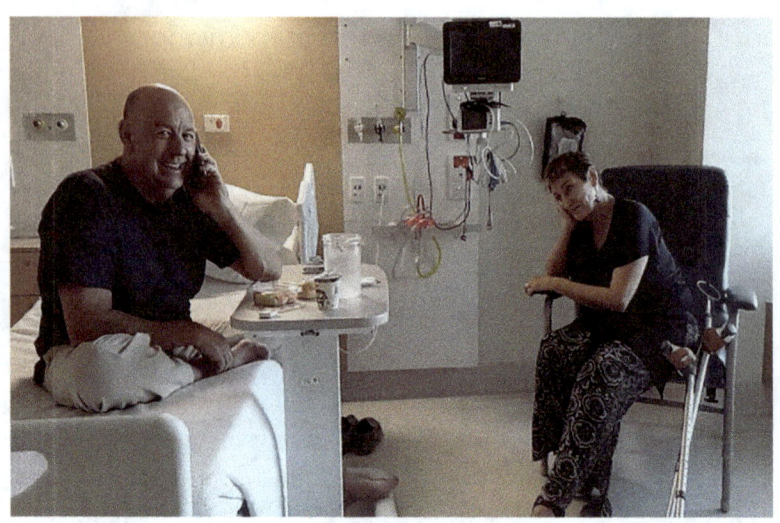

9th February 2018

Geoff adds, "When I got installed in the Cardiac ward, I was just thinking about the next morning, whether I could eat or not and when I'd have a wash. I called all the kids to let them know where I was and what was about to happen, at last. A Cardiac ward doctor came in to check on me and asked, 'Why are you smiling so much?' and I answered, 'Because I'm excited about getting a new heart tomorrow morning!'"

"Toni and you Eve were with me when, to my surprise, Robert came in to tell me he would be the surgeon operating on me after all. It turned out that Chris Merry was already scheduled for another operation at the same time. So, Robert was to do it after all. I was so happy."

Robert briefed Geoff on the operation schedule, noting the 5 % risk of death during the procedure that he was obliged to state for patient consent. This didn't take the smile off Geoff's face. At this point, Toni's own heart was beating rapidly with anxiety, but her drugs were keeping her reactions slightly suppressed. She vividly recalls, "Emotionally, I was feeling the enormity of the event, but I felt relatively calm because Geoff was so happy and positive, and because Robert was in charge with an experienced, capable team."

Geoff's positivity was truly contagious. We were somewhat less anxious because he was expressing such genuine joy and calm excitement. He really was very grounded and centred and we knew he was in the best hands with Robert and the Fiona Stanley medical team.

Chapter Forty Seven

A most momentous day!

Geoff recalls, "I don't remember if I ate anything at all that evening. I had to fast for the next morning, 10th February, and I was eventually wheeled out on the gurney at about 8.00 am, and left in the corridor as the transplant team assembled. I eventually had a canula put in my arm by the anaesthetist. I was very excited, getting wheeled in and transferred to the operating table.

"I was saying goodbye to all my surroundings, as I entered the dark space, the void, the nothing – and what seemed an instant, 24-hours later – still in the blackness, a distant voice was asking me to cough. I had all these tubes down my throat. Until I could demonstrate a cough reflex, they weren't going to remove them because I could drown in my own fluids. I had a couple of attempts to cough, but it seemed to go on for hours. Robert assured me later, it was only about nine minutes. I was totally powerless to do anything except attempt a pathetic little cough. So, when I was successful at that, the tubes were pulled out, and suddenly I was in the room, coming-to, out of the void. Then as I was having my blood pressure taken, I could see how normal it was, and suddenly realised *I HAD A NEW HEART*! I celebrated in my head, as best I could, as Toni and Eve showed up.

"However, as I became more physically aware, I felt like I

was coming out of a car crash. Nothing felt normal. My chest felt very tight but I was still so drugged up that I felt weird. Everything was taped up, so I couldn't see my wound. Over the next 24 hours, I had constant medico visits and lots of checks. On day one I was invited to stand up, and that was an event in itself. On day two, I was wheeled down to the gym for a very light workout. Eleven days later, I was sent home. Yay, how exciting!"

However, before Geoff's release, there was another challenging new reality at home. Toni was dealing with her repaired knee, and her prescribed drugs. I took carer's leave from work to stay with her for a week. Toni could not clean or cook, and was barely mobile, even with crutches. She tried using a walker, but that didn't serve her well. She was having a lot of trouble with her medications, needed for severe nerve pain, but they typically did not suit her body or state of mind. She was very concerned about their addictive qualities too.

Consequently, I had to drive the pair of us around to different doctors, some 'out of hours', in her desire to reduce the drugs, increase them again, change them, delete them, and so on. Each excursion required me to get Toni in and out of the car, still needing to be placed along the back seat with her pills, crutches and handbag in tow. She was constantly sliding between 'highs' and 'lows', and experiencing pain. In between, she cautiously, but regularly, did all of her assigned exercises. Whether she was high or low – but mostly high – her phone was in use most of the time. She was either making calls to Geoff, or receiving calls from him. Otherwise, she was making calls to family and friends, or receiving calls from them inquiring about her and Geoff at the same time. It was all quite a roller coaster ride for us both.

Over time, family and friends generously provided cooked

dishes or helped to clean for Toni. Their friend, Heather, kindly generated a roster of duties too. Sometimes a simple visit provided welcome company to the housebound patient. Of course, Toni and I visited Geoff throughout his hospital recovery, following our usual transport routine.

Robyn and a few of Geoff's friends assisted in ways concerning Geoff's photography business, but they needed urgent access to his computer. The main problem was that Geoff often changed his master password, and sometimes forgot it, as he had at that time. In his condition, in hospital, it was difficult to keep questioning him, urging him to remember. What a seriously stressful task that was for all involved.

Robert kept in regular communication with Toni about Geoff's medical condition and progress, including information about what to expect during his recovery process. He also regularly checked on her own physical and emotional welfare. Their other close medico friends kindly checked on her welfare too. Drugs were still an issue because of her nerve pain. However, she soon reduced them until she could cope with just Panadol, so her mental state became more balanced.

Chapter Forty Eight

Meanwhile in ICU

In contrast, while in Fiona Stanley with a brand new heart, Geoff was having his own drug-related issues.

"Initially, in recovery from Day 1 to Day 3, I had drug-induced dreams. I kept seeing the same things, like I was on a movie set, and nothing was real. This happened three nights in a row. Finally, I pressed the call button and two nurses came in, only to find me leaning against the bed, having pulled my tubes out. There was a mess everywhere and they said, 'Geoff, what are you doing?' I think I must have had a sheepish look on my face. But I still didn't trust them because they were the main characters in my paranoid dreams. Even after wakening, I still believed those nurses were fakes. But they were able to get me back into bed and reconnect the drug lines. They spent quite some time working out how to get the right quantity of drugs feeding into me again.

"Apart from that drama, the drugs induced the most amazing visual effects that I enjoyed every time I closed my eyes. I was entertained by beautiful works of art of my own creation. I wished I could record them to make them real. The walls kept moving and I saw fascinating patterns rolling past all the time. I would see a person, a face, and then it would morph into something else. At one stage I saw a complete tip-truck made of red house bricks. I dreamed in so much detail.

I could also make things up, beginning with gorgeous colours and seeing one picture turn into another. I could be looking at a person in a sepia tone and suddenly it morphed into a dog, then something else. I liked that experience – it was all totally legal and the drugs were free, thanks to Medicare! The visions stopped when they changed the drugs.

"In recovery, lying on the bed, my new heart seemed to be thumping with my whole body shaking. I had forgotten what it was like to have such a strong beating heart in my chest. I decided at the time that it was like putting a 5-litre V8 motor into a Volkswagen Beetle. That was a bit unnerving at times, but I was very happy, and celebrating the fact that it was doing such a good job already. All the time, I was testing how I felt and how different I was feeling, and checking to see if I really was better than I had been over the previous ten years or so. I was told not to cough, and I had to do exercises without bursting stitches, so I felt I was in a cocoon and unable to fully test my new heart. There were many moments when I felt elated as I progressively felt better. I think my brain activity also improved with better oxygen flow too."

Chapter Forty Nine

The good and the bad of post-op

"Then it was time to exercise, so I walked around the ward as often as I could manage with a stainless-steel trolley in front of me for balance. I still had the same attitude – if I was told to do two laps, I'd do ten. Just sitting in bed wasn't much fun and I didn't like the food. I decided that the kitchen was trying to poison me with the coffee, because my taste buds had deserted me. The coffee tasted like rusty water that had been in a forty-four gallon drum for a couple of years. If I managed to get hold of some sushi rolls, they tasted terrible, even though they looked good. If I had a chocolate, or something sweet like that, it tasted crappy. It took me nine months to get my sense of taste back.

"Part of my right hand was numb for about six months, but the medicos didn't seem to worry about these things. They seemed to think these functions would come back. In my initial recovery, the hardest part was that I wasn't allowed to use my arms to sit up - which was impossible - or to move around in the bed. They were worried about me messing up my ribcage, because they had cut me down the sternum to open me up for the heart, in a clam shell fashion. I knew it was all wired up. As I progressed, I asked all the medicos when I'd be allowed to have a swim, and they said 'in six weeks'.

"I was home on day eleven, which was fantastic, and this was earlier than most recipients, although they try to get people out of the hospital as quickly as possible these days. My eleven days went quickly, but not without little dramas, mostly drug-related.

"Anything can happen with complications, but fortunately, I had a dream run! Every reading of my liver and other organs, and other vital signs were good. The medical team were very happy with my outcome. So ... Robert did a great job on me! My experience was that the ablations were worse than the transplant."

On Geoff's return home, many friends, including his water polo and swimming team mates, continued to offer welcome help and company. Geoff and Toni were both very grateful, and were touched by their friendship.

With gratitude, Geoff adds, "One of the best things about my recovery, post-op, was that there were no more fibrillations. No more arrhythmias. No more pacemaker or defibrillator. All gone ... out with the old and in with the new! Any pain in recovery was definitely worth it and not my concern. Robert did not allow me to forget that I had to take all my drugs consistently, that I had to 'love my pills' three times a day, every day. So, I always have my watch alarm set for the same three times a day. And I do love my pills!"

Doctors thought that his legs would be weaker post-transplant, due to his immobilised state in hospital. For any patient, loss of tone and a degree of muscular atrophy can occur, but they were also concerned that Geoff's normal leg weakness would be exacerbated. He was constantly urged to keep exercising his legs – he had to practise sitting down and rising from a chair with his arms folded over his chest, progressing to stretching his arms out in front of him.

Both Geoff and Toni were also warned that when Geoff came home, he could be wildly manic, expressed as talking and eating excessively, due to the steroids he would be on initially. That was a bit alarming as we thought we could receive an out-of-control version of Geoff, with particular concern about potential for extreme eating. We thought we would just have to weather the storm! Fortunately, as it happened, he was quite normal and happy. Steroids normally cause puffiness, mainly in the face and neck, and he experienced a little of that for a short while.

Geoff's drugs still affected his capacity to taste and smell normally, which may have dampened any chemical drive to eat more. He could not enjoy eating or drinking his favourite things, even chocolate, ice-cream, wine, and coffee, previously unheard of! As he remembers, "Most things tasted bad."

This was frustrating, difficult and disappointing for Geoff, as it also was for Toni, who enjoys cooking for an enthusiastic husband — their usual dynamic. However, Toni was less productive in the kitchen, while managing her own painful knee.

Toni agrees with Geoff about their situation: "Neither of us could drive. We were stuck at home, dealing with each other's ailments and our own frustrations, so we were both very grateful for visits from family, friends and team mates."

Post-transplant biopsies

Geoff explains, "Post-operatively, programmed biopsies to detect rejection were performed every week, then every fortnight, then three monthly, then six monthly. Now I have to have them twelve-monthly. They involve making a cut on the right side of the neck and sending a pincer wire, called a bioptome, through the jugular vein to the heart muscle, taking a tiny chunk to analyse. The biopsies take about thirty minutes to complete. All of my biopsies have shown zero sign of rejection."

When I expressed my sympathy about the discomfort of these regular biopsies, he replied, as he had about other painful incidents in the past, "It's just pain – I don't focus on it … and I enjoy these biopsy procedures, in spite of the fact that my wife says that is a ridiculous thing to say. I think it is good to find out that everything is okay – and I probably just love the attention. I get a cup of coffee and a sandwich afterwards. I get to lie around for a morning and answer the same questions a hundred times. Every time they ask me if I've fallen over in the last twelve months, I lie through my teeth and say, 'No, I don't know what you're talking about.' But I admit here, I fell over in the driveway, tripping over my own feet and rolling on the paving stones. That's just because of my legs, not my heart. Anyway, my legs are getting stronger every day, so imagine how strong they'll be in twenty years!"

Pills

Geoff has had to spend an inordinate amount of time attending to his pill regime post op at home. He has maintained a system of sitting down at the dining table with a huge Webster Pack and his vast range of pills, while referring to a pill schedule chart. He cannot be interrupted when he is attending to this vital sorting task.

The pill challenge alone has been massive. Astonishing us all, he has been able to swallow twenty pills at a time – nothing like efficiency! He has taken them without any complaint, sticking to his new mantra of, "I love my pills." Fortunately, he now takes many less pills, but he still has his watch alarm set to keep them regular. Occasionally a drug is changed to one that doesn't suit him and needs to be changed again, but he is always prepared to go with the pill flow. There are potential, common side effects from the drugs, including skin cancer and diabetes. A few skin cancers have had to be excised, which Geoff has managed with his usual stoicism.

As for Geoff's bees, after being stung one-too-many-times, including a rushed trip to hospital when his tongue swelled up, his doctors advised him to give them up, considering his risk of anaphylaxis. He had never had any problems in the past. We wondered if the bees were reacting to particular pheromones emitted through his skin, due to his drugs.

Geoff, the beekeeper, in honey heaven

Chapter Fifty

Joy

"I was told that I wasn't allowed to go into the water before six weeks. That waiting period ended on a Sunday. I got up early and drove straight to Beatty Park, where I had the gentlest swim that you could possibly imagine. I swam across the water polo pool where the guys and girls were training.

"I wanted to see how swimming again was going to work, and it was fine, but I was taking it very carefully, stroke by stroke. I had been told many times to take care with my wired up sternum – which always shows up on x-rays.

"My chest was sore, but it was getting better all the time. I was told to take it easy, and I did for quite some time! Now the highlight of a swim might be a few half-laps of butterfly. They tell me the heart needs to work harder from time to time, as it's a muscle. I rely on hormones in the blood to speed up my heart because I have no vagus nerve connection to the brain. The vagus nerve cannot be reconnected to a new heart. I was advised to warm up and cool down slowly, otherwise, I wouldn't feel very well, but so far I've been fine. And even now, when I lean over, I'm excited to know that I don't feel faint – after ten years of feeling I would collapse because of insufficient circulation and low blood pressure from heart failure."

When Robert showed Geoff and Toni a scan of Geoff's old heart, compared with his new heart, they were shocked. Toni described it as, "His old heart was enlarged and floppy, like the wings of a dying butterfly. The new heart is proportioned and sitting in the right place."

Post-transplant Geoff getting his tone back, 2018

Seeing the stark difference in his heart, and thinking about what this meant for him, Geoff comments, "While I was swimming with Shane McGurk's group recently, I remembered when my original cardiac specialist, Mark Ireland, told me early on, that I wasn't to swim alone any more with my old heart, and how hard that was to hear. But now I feel safe and free!"

Old habits

Concerning other delights, Geoff adds, "It took nine months for my taste buds to come back." He still likes a hunk of crusty bread – most of which is baked by his wife – deliciously supporting layers of butter and honey or cheese, accompanied with fresh cream in his coffee, and so it goes … New heart, but same old Geoff!

Chapter Fifty One

Reflections

"My parents' health problems could be part of my story, as we are born with certain predispositions to certain illnesses. My mother had atherosclerosis which affected her heart. She had to get a pig's valve replacement, but died of a heart arrest a week before she turned sixty-two. And my maternal grandfather, Arthur Mardon, died of a heart attack, aged sixty-two. His out-of-wedlock son in England died at sixty-one of heart disease too. I don't know what my maternal grandmother died of, or when exactly. My father had gout, but died of liver cancer, aged sixty-six. Working in the mines could have contributed to this, but drinking and smoking wouldn't have helped. And I had my heart arrest at sixty-one!"

Robyn added, "I was desperate to get to sixty-two years of age, to get past the 'sixty-one' hurdle. Unfortunately, I don't know anything much about my paternal grandfather's or grandmother's lives or illnesses."

Research shows their paternal grandfather was Thomas William Fisher, born 8 June 1871. In 1909, he married Nellie Wypie, born 13 December 1879. They were both born and married, and died in County Durham. The family lived at 5 Hall Gardens, Boldon, Durham. The 1939 Census shows that Thomas was a coal miner and Nellie had home duties. During the census, they still had two sons residing with them: James H. R., born 1 February 1916 and Albert H. born 29 February 1920. Thomas died as a pensioner in 1952 aged 80, if research details are correct. Nellie died in 1969, aged 90. Apparently, Nellie's maiden name of Wypie was originally spelt Ypey, with Dutch origins. When I relayed this information to Geoff, he said, "Oh, well, I guess that's where I got my arrogance from, haha!"

Yet, Geoff is happy to learn that his paternal grandparents lived long lives, and hopes to even improve on their record, thanks to his new heart, adding, "I'm just lucky to have been given a second chance, brought about by circumstances that were controlled by some highly trained, skilled people. I swim with a heart surgeon, a cardiologist, a G.P. and an anaesthetist – and although I was married once to a doctor, I'm now married and sleep with a naturopath. If my cardiac arrest happened when I was alone, or with different people around me, I could have just been a little note in history and everyone would have been managing without me" … while Toni interjects, "No, we wouldn't, we wouldn't manage at all …", and Geoff tags, "… and both my friends would have just gone on doing what they always do!"

Geoff continues, "I met Robert when he came to me for family photos in 2002. Consequently, we became firm friends and as Robert was a swimmer, I introduced him to water polo. I respect Robert a lot. I think he's an amazing person – not just for his awesome surgical skills. He carries great responsibility, which can weigh heavily at times. He works with a dedicated transplant team and other medical staff who are under maximum pressure for very long hours. He is on call day and night, much of the time. He is a committed advocate for the Donate Life program for organ donation, to which he gives a great amount of his own time, and through which I was able to receive my own new heart. He's always available to help people in need. He is a very generous, caring person.

"As for any concerns about the transplant operation, of course I thought I could die on the table. I learned later that my new heart was initially difficult to get started, but Robert didn't tell me that at the time. Of course, I was a bit concerned about the outcome, that if I had a problem as a result of the operation, Rob might feel bad about it. But that's the risk you take anyway, and I'd rather take that risk with someone who I knew had my best interests at heart.

"And as for my family, I realise Toni had a great deal of anxiety from 2009. Taking my old heart out and putting a new one in definitely had risks and I don't underestimate the impact of that. The kids were anxious too. I was happy to call them to let them know about everything, but I couldn't do more, and I realise that was probably hard for them.

"Since the op, I've been exercising regularly, swimming four times a week in the mornings, which is great, and catching up with swimming friends. Within the first year, I was an honorary member of a girls' water polo team, 'The Pink Pointers'. They called me 'Geoffrina!' and were very encouraging. I also use my rowing machine at home. I gave my racing bike to Jasmine because of my legs, and the potential for accidents."

Chapter Fifty Two

Donate Life and donors

"I think a lot about the heart donor and the family, about how I got a new heart that saved my life, how the donation was borne out of their tragedy. At first, I actually felt guilty and maybe a bit selfish, that my joy was someone else's sadness. Before I got the heart, I wondered about potential donors, like accident victims, and how their hearts could go to someone else like me – then I felt guilty for even thinking about it. It was a weird conflict that still haunts me occasionally. I am so grateful. I feel so fortunate. As I said before, I am lucky to have a second chance. I would like people to give up their superstitions about donating organs. People need to be real about it, as a community, but it's a family decision to donate, of course.

"The Donate Life Foundation does the most amazing work. They are dedicated to saving lives through organ donation. They protect the donor families' privacy, but recipients can write letters to the 'unknown' families and request communication. I have written to my donor family a couple of times expressing a wish to thank them personally, but they have not responded. I accept that. I really respect that it is the families' right to not respond."

"About Donate Life, I believe that everyone should have a conversation with their family about donating organs. It's a generous thing to do, and something a rational person could expect. I think that to take your organs to the grave or the incinerator is selfish."

Early days for a deeply grateful recipient

Chapter Fifty Three

Music's in the heart

"It wasn't until I was seventy-one, that I decided to take some formal piano lessons – which is where I am now – a beginner. Lessons are great. The degree of difficulty, co-ordinating both sides of the brain with focus is a good challenge."

Geoff's music dating back to 1988

Geoff has also re-started flute lessons, picking up where he left off in the past. His harmonica still gets a little workout in spontaneous bursts.

Geoff comments, "I think of missed opportunities. I would have liked to have learnt piano when I was young, but I'm pleased to take it on in my 70s, and for the rest of my life. There's a spiritual element to music. Even listening to choirs and choral pieces takes my mind into the realm of my higher self, which is fascinating. It reminds me of my better self and makes me want to do good things for my family, my community and the world at large.

"Music takes me to other places. It heightens my sense of creativity. When I was a photographer for the West Australian newspaper, working on a farm during holidays to make extra money, I listened to classical music from 7 am to 7 pm. I tried to compose symphonies in my head. I'd get lost driving tractors down dusty paddocks as music blared on cab speakers. Listening to music, I leave my troubles behind.

"I'm proud of my grandfather's musical legacy. I'm proud that he was so accomplished. He made it his life, but it came first, before his family. He had the camaraderie of his fellow bandsmen and a lot of success, but I suspect his family came second."

Chapter Fifty Four

Life post-transplant

"After the transplant, I was introduced to a lot of powerful medications, including the immuno-suppressant drugs that I have to take for the rest of my life to survive. I have been warned all the way along that I must be careful about contracting anything infectious from other people because of this, so with Covid 19 I had to stop shaking hands and hugging. Toni has had to take more precautions than before, too."

However, a healthy heart meant a special freedom became possible. Toni and Geoff were able to visit Emma and Jasmine and their children in Melbourne over the 2020 Christmas period, while this biography was being written. They had a wonderful visit, but had to isolate on their return home for fourteen days, including getting a Covid test in the process — all expected, so no complaints there. They had a wonderful time meeting Emma's and Jasmine's partners, Adam and Ky, rejuvenating precious face-to-face, tactile bonds with growing grandsons, Charlie, Max and Forrest, and generally sharing love and fun with all of them at their homes.

It was the first time Geoff and Toni had seen Emma with young Charlie and Max, and partner Adam, as well as Jasmine with little Forrest, and partner Ky, since before Geoff's transplant. The last time they met, Geoff was seriously ill with an uncertain future. Now, Geoff's new heart is full … and

Toni's is much more content.

Chapter Fifty Five

A message to my children and grandchildren

"I would like my children to know it is important to have a good sense of humour and to live each day, to enjoy life, rather than just to get through it. Sometimes life is just like 'Groundhog Day', so we have to reach out above and beyond 'the everyday'. It's important to focus on our children, enough to let them know we are around, that we are interested in what they're doing. But we can't hang on to them the whole time. We must let them do their own thing, so they develop their own personalities, and resilience. I hope my grandchildren grow up with a strong sense of self. This might mean taking the road less travelled."

About this, Emma commented. "I am really grateful to Dad for allowing us free will as we grew up, as I think it is important for children to be able to find out who they are and what they want to do in life, unhampered by parental expectations and restrictions."

Geoff continues, "I'd also like them all to know the whole story about my heart journey – what I did, how I felt, and the outcomes. I hope they learn not to give in to difficult events. I hope they learn to encourage and support other people who might go through similar life events, with injury, illness, heart or other problems, as well as depression and suicidal thoughts, and knowing that there are always people who love you, and all you have to do is reach out to ask for help."

Geoff's humour has been a constant feature of his expression and colours all his interactions with others. Fortunately, nothing has changed over time on that front. Yet, as a mature person, Geoff acknowledges that, at times, 'dark clouds cloud humour'. Nevertheless, with the devoted support of his wife Toni and his family and many friends – and some therapy when needed – he has always returned to his positive default mindset, actively seeking the funny, curious and beautiful, usually finding good in others with his alternative ways of perceiving events and the world at large.

Chapter Fifty Six

Covid 19 and more reflection

In Australia since early 2020, the population has experienced the Covid 19 pandemic. Western Australia initially kept a 'closed border' to the other states and internationally, so there was a period of time when Victoria (home state of daughters' families) was in constant lockdowns with very high case levels. Although W.A. was practically Covid-free, the sad irony was that Geoff had received a new life-giving heart and was feeling healthy again – but being immuno-suppressed to help prevent heart rejection, travelling presented some risk. However, he and Toni were greatly missing being with their daughters and grandsons, as so many other people were in Australia. So, a window of opportunity at Christmas 2020, kindly facilitated by their daughters and partners, was a special gift.

Geoff's sister Janis commented that their mother Jessie was born in 1918 when the Spanish Flu pandemic was in Australia and which proliferated in 1919 after Peace Day celebrations. Later, in the 1950s, the Poliomyelitis pandemic severely impacted Australians too. As Covid has also reached Hawaii, Janis noted, "Here we are 100 years later with three generations of Fishers and Mardons, facing our own pandemic."

Geoff comments further, "Now I sadly reflect on my

family history, asking myself, 'Why didn't I sit down with my mother and father and actually ask them about their lives, their histories?' I wonder how they felt about World War II. I feel cheated by the arrival of television and the way it cut off our family conversations and story-telling. I admire families who can resist the constant bombardment of outside influences and discuss their day-to-day issues and politics. But I still remember my father's warning about '... those Communists'.

"Now in my later years, I reflect more. I feel a little ashamed of myself that, as a young adult, I was too concerned with my own life to inquire about my own family history. But it's never too late. While I still draw breath and stand on my two skinny, nerve-damaged legs, I will take more interest in other people than in my own life challenges. Long live my unrealistic expectations …

"And may I give full recognition and express my love and gratitude to my wife Toni, my partner in life – warm, creative, flexible and adventurous, and always supportive through everything, to all my loving, fun, interesting and evolving family, to all my good friends and important people around me who have cared for me and kept me alive. Also, special thanks to my friend Robert who has saved me twice – throwing steaks on the barbecue one week, and giving me a new heart a week later. What a legend!"

Unofficial Leo friends' club! Toni, Geoff, Robert, Claire and Gary Ward

A few extra family pics

More youthful days for Geoff, Toni, Robyn, Eve

Australia Day family picnic – Toni, Geoff, Anne and Eve
Matilda Bay   2005

Geoff, Toni, Eve – Attadale 2021

Some of Geoff's arty photos

Richard Syme 2020

Brendan Fisher, 2019

'Special Assistant' Jasmine in her school uniform with her pet rats.

Ashley baking at Bread In Common, Fremantle, 2019

Venice

Street performer, Venice

Nannup trees

NOT THE END!

www.ingramcontent.com/pod-product-compliance
Lightning Source LLC
Chambersburg PA
CBHW070502120526
44590CB00013B/727